REGENTS RESTORATION DRAMA SERIES

General Editor: John Loftis

THE HISTORICAL REGISTER
FOR THE YEAR 1736
and
EURYDICE HISSED

HENRY FIELDING

The Historical Register
For the Year 1736

and

Eurydice Hissed

Edited by

WILLIAM W. APPLETON

LONDON
EDWARD ARNOLD (PUBLISHERS) LTD.

Board edition: SBN 7131 5405 5
Paper edition: SBN 7131 5406 3

Printed in Great Britain by
William Clowes and Sons, Limited, London and Beccles

Regents Restoration Drama Series

The Regents Restoration Drama Series, similar in objectives and format to the Regents Renaissance Drama Series, will provide soundly edited texts, in modern spelling, of the more significant English plays of the late seventeenth and early eighteenth centuries. The word "Restoration" is here used ambiguously and must be explained. If to the historian it refers to the period between 1660 and 1685 (or 1688), it has long been used by the student of drama in default of a more precise word to refer to plays belonging to the dramatic tradition established in the 1660's, weakening after 1700, and displaced in the 1730's. It is in this extended sense—imprecise though justified by academic custom—that the word is used in this series, which will include plays first produced between 1660 and 1737. Although these limiting dates are determined by political events, the return of Charles II (and the removal of prohibitions against the operation of theaters) and the passage of Walpole's Stage Licensing Act, they enclose a period of dramatic history having a coherence of its own in the establishment, development, and disintegration of a tradition.

Each text in the series is based on a fresh collation of the seventeenth- and eighteenth-century editions that might be presumed to have authority. The textual notes, which appear above the rule at the bottom of each page, record all substantive departures from the edition used as the copy-text. Variant substantive readings among contemporary editions are listed there as well. Editions later than the eighteenth century are referred to in the textual notes only when an emendation originating in some one of them is received into the text. Variants of accidentals (spelling, punctuation, capitalization) are not recorded in the notes. Contracted forms of characters' names are silently expanded in speech prefixes and stage directions, and, in the case of speech prefixes, are regularized. Additions to the stage directions of the copy-text are enclosed in brackets. Stage directions such as "within" or "aside" are enclosed in parentheses when they occur in the copy-text.

Spelling has been modernized along consciously conservative lines, but within the limits of a modernized text the linguistic quality of the original has been carefully preserved. Contracted preterites have regularly been expanded. Punctuation has been brought into accord with modern practices. The objective has been to achieve a balance between the pointing of the old editions and a system of punctuation which, without overloading the text with exclamation marks, semicolons, and dashes, will make the often loosely flowing verse and prose of the original syntactically intelligible to the modern reader. Dashes are regularly used only to indicate interrupted speeches, or shifts of address within a single speech.

Explanatory notes, chiefly concerned with glossing obsolete words and phrases, are printed below the textual notes at the bottom of each page. References to stage directions in the notes follow the admirable system of the Revels editions, whereby stage directions are keyed, decimally, to the line of the text before or after which they occur. Thus, a note on 0.2 has reference to the second line of the stage direction at the beginning of the scene in question. A note on 115.1 has reference to the first line of the stage direction following line 115 of the text of the relevant scene. Speech prefixes, and any stage directions attached to them, are keyed to the first line of accompanying dialogue.

JOHN LOFTIS

Stanford University

Contents

List of Abbreviations

A   *8vo.*, London, Roberts [1737].

B   *8vo.*, Dublin, Risk, 1737.

C   *12mo.*, Dublin, Jones, 1737.

D   *8vo.*, London, Watts, 1741.

E   *8vo.*, "Third Edition," London, Bickerton, 1744.

F   *4to.*, *Works* (ed. Arthur Murphy), London, Millar, 1762.

Ap   *8vo.*, London, Roberts [1737] [piracy].

OED   *Oxford English Dictionary*

Introduction

There is only one bibliographical problem connected with *The Historical Register for the Year 1736* and *Eurydice Hissed*. In his work on Henry Fielding, Wilbur Cross recorded two editions "Printed: and Sold by J. Roberts," both undated, one with 41 pages of text for the two plays and the other with 48 pages.[1] Contemporary notices in *The Grub St. Journal* and *The London Evening Post* specify May 12, 1737, as the date of publication for the two plays. In Cross' opinion the 41-page edition appeared on that date and the 48-page edition, "the 2d edition, though not so named," at a later date.

There are now substantial reasons for believing that the 48-page edition (subsequently referred to as the A text) is the true first edition and the 41-page text (subsequently referred to as Ap) is, in fact, a piracy.[2] The primary evidence for this conclusion is based on recent studies of printers' devices. The ornaments found in A appear regularly in the books printed for Roberts, while those in Ap do not, but do appear regularly in the books printed by William Cheyne of Edinburgh.[3]

Further evidence supports the conclusion that Ap is an unauthorized edition. Text A and text Ap were set up independently, a procedure which would have resulted in unnecessary expense for Roberts since the variants between the two are compositorial and not substantive and errors could easily have been corrected without a complete re-setting. That the A text is the accepted text of the play no one has disputed. It served as the copy-text for subsequent editions published both in London and Dublin, and the variant readings in Ap, in every case inferior to those in A, are evidently the errors of a careless compositor.

Still other arguments substantiate the primacy of the A text. The scarcity of copies of Ap has long puzzled Fielding collectors. First editions of *Pasquin*, Fielding's great success of the previous year, are

---

[1] Wilbur L. Cross, *The History of Henry Fielding* (Yale, 1918), III, 301–302.

[2] A collates A–D^8; Ap collates Π8($-\Pi$8) A–E^4 F^1($=\Pi$8).

[3] I am indebted for this information to Professor David Foxon of Queen's College, Ontario.

relatively common. *The Historical Register* and *Eurydice Hissed* enjoyed an equal success, yet copies of Ap are almost nonexistent, although copies of A turn up fairly frequently. A reversal of the previously accepted order of texts in Cross' bibliography would explain this discrepancy. Such a reversal would also explain the otherwise curiously named "third edition" issued by Bickerton in 1744. Bickerton was evidently either unaware of or unconcerned with the two Dublin editions of Fielding's plays. He did, however, know of one edition printed for Roberts in 1737 and of one printed for Watts in 1741. Eager to take advantage of Fielding's recent popularity as the author of *Joseph Andrews*, Bickerton bought from Roberts a number of sets of unsold sheets of the A text and re-issued them with a fresh title page, designating the edition as the "third," and crediting Fielding, for the first time, as the author.

All texts between 1737 and 1762 are based upon the A text, which is also the copy-text for this edition.

The Historical Register for the Year 1736 is familiar, by name at least, to many readers. In almost every survey of English drama it gets passing mention as a play which proved a major factor in bringing about the Licensing Act of 1737. Its importance in this context has perhaps been overrated, but it is Henry Fielding's most entertaining play.

If a modern reader finds himself bewildered by this patchwork entertainment, with its glancing allusions to politics, society, and the theater, he can take some comfort from the fact that it puzzled Fielding's contemporaries as well.[4] Although patterned after Buckingham's *The Rehearsal*, with its central device of a play within a play, it does not fit comfortably into the genre of the dramatic burlesque.[5] Fielding himself preferred to describe it as a "dramatic satire," a term which he casually defines in *The Historical Register* as a mixture of several plots, "some pretty deep and some but shallow," designed to "divert the town and bring full houses." He had first attempted the species in *The Author's Farce* (1730) and subsequently experimented with it in *Tom Thumb* (1730) and the enormously successful *Pasquin* (1736). His first editor, Arthur Murphy, put these plays into

[4] Typical is Colley Cibber who in his *Apology* (London, 1740), p. 164, describes Fielding's plays as "pieces of an extraordinary kind."

[5] Dane Smith, *Plays about the Theatre 1671–1737* (Oxford, 1936), pp. 220–231.

still another category.[6] Their pungency, topicality, and unabashed personal satire, he decided, related them above all to Aristophanic comedy, and indeed, with the sole exception of Samuel Foote, Henry Fielding is the only dramatist in eighteenth-century England recognizably within the Aristophanic tradition.[7]

Regardless of the term used to describe them, these short plays show Henry Fielding, the dramatist, at his best. The looseness of their structure worked to his advantage in giving free play to his wit and imagination. On his more serious comedies, patterned after those of Congreve, he lavished time and effort but, paradoxically, he showed off his youthful talents far more effectively in these unpretentious entertainments, dashed off at journalistic speed. If we are to believe Arthur Murphy, they were often scribbled on bits of tobacco-paper, late at night, after a convivial evening in a tavern,[8] and in *Eurydice Hissed* Fielding boasts of "writing nine scenes with spirit in one day." It is this spontaneity and ebullience which give these short plays their freshness and appeal. At the modest Little Theatre in the Haymarket, known as Mr. Fielding's scandal-shop, he knocked "all distinctions of mankind on the head: religion, laws, government, priests, judges, and ministers were all laid flat at the feet of this Herculean satirist!"[9] His entertainments were, in short, the predecessors of the intimate satirical revue—topical, iconoclastic, and witty.[10]

The Little Theatre in the Haymarket was the ideal showcase for such entertainments. There, in 1730, Fielding had produced *Tom Thumb*, and there, six years later, his troupe, facetiously known as the Great Mogul's Company, had presented *Pasquin*. Like any ambitious young playwright, Fielding was first drawn to Drury Lane, but his muse was clearly ill at ease in that house. In January of 1737 he and his friend James Ralph, the journalist, reassembled the Great Mogul's Company for a further season at the Little Theatre.[11] They

6 Arthur Murphy, ed., *Works of Henry Fielding* (London, 1762), I, 12. See also F. W. Bateson, *English Comic Drama 1700–1750* (Oxford, 1929), p. 121.

7 Fielding and Edward Young's translation of Aristophanes' *Plutus, God of Riches* was published in 1742.

8 Ed., *Works*, I, 26–27.

9 Cibber, *Apology*, p. 164.

10 *Beyond the Fringe*, a recent example of the genre, is clearly within the tradition of Fielding's dramatic satires.

11 Emmett L. Avery, "Fielding's Last Season with the Haymarket Theatre," *Modern Philology*, XXXVII (1939), 283–292.

inaugurated it with two plays, now lost, *The Defeat of Apollo* and *The Fall of Bob, alias Gin,* one satirizing the taste for pantomimes and the other, presumably, the unpopular Gin Act of 1736.[12] *The Historical Register* was first announced in early March. Originally, it seems, Fielding proposed to combine it in a double bill with a now-lost comedy, *The Rehearsal of Kings.*[13] But he had second thoughts about this. On February 19 his farce of *Eurydice* had ignominiously failed at Drury Lane. Shortly thereafter he composed a "short and very merry farce called *The Damnation of Eurydice,*" and on March 15 he announced that it would be performed with *The Historical Register.*[14] But once again he changed his mind, and at the last moment he substituted for *The Damnation of Eurydice* George Lillo's bourgeois tragedy, *Fatal Curiosity.*[15]

The preliminary advertisement for *The Historical Register,* which was first performed on March 21, 1737, reads as follows:

A new dramatic satire: with freshest advices foreign and domestic. Written by the author of *Pasquin . . .* in the boxes at 5s.; in the pit at 3s.; in the gallery at 2s. Note, none will be admitted after the house is full; for which reason, the sooner you come, or secure your places, the better. All persons are desired to cry at the tragedy and laugh at the comedy, being quite contrary to the general practice.[16]

Its success was immediate and unequivocal. On the following day Egmont recorded in his diary: "It is a good satire on the times and has a good deal of wit,"[17] and *The Daily Advertiser* enthusiastically observed: "Last night the two new performances at the Haymarket . . . were received with the greatest applause ever shown at the theatre."[18] So profitable did this double bill prove that it continued to be played until April 13 when the retitled *Eurydice Hissed* replaced Lillo's play. Once again Egmont attended and approved:

12 *Ibid.* Avery speculates on the possibility that Fielding had a hand in these plays.

13 Cross, *Fielding,* I, 209, suggests that this may have been an old play revised by Fielding.

14 See *The Daily Advertiser* of that date.

15 Lillo's play had its first performance on May 27, 1736, at the Little Theatre in the Haymarket.

16 *The Daily Advertiser,* March 21, 1737, quoted in Arthur H. Scouten, *The London Stage, Part 3: 1729–1747* (Carbondale, Illinois, 1961), II, 651.

17 John Perceval, Earl of Egmont, *Diary* (London, 1920–1923), II, 375.

18 *The Daily Advertiser,* March 22, 1737.

"To the Haymarket playhouse where a farce was acted called
Eurydice First [*Hissed*] an allegory on the loss of the Excise Bill. The
whole was a satire on Sir Robert Walpole, and I observed that when
any strong passages fell, the Prince [Frederick] who was there,
clapped, especially when in favor of liberty." [19]

Fielding was undoubtedly encouraged by his patrons, Chesterfield
and Lyttelton, leading members of the opposition to the Ministry, to
make Walpole the chief butt of *The Historical Register*, but he also had
other satiric targets in view: "a pack of patriots, a pack of ladies [and]
a pack of beaux." [20] Though he drew his title from a publication of
that name which had been appearing since 1716, his play is anything
but "an impartial relation of all transactions, foreign and domestic,"
as that work advertised itself, nor did he attempt any serious com-
ment on the vast international power struggle being played out on
the chessboard of Europe. [21]

Society, the theater, and politics are equally the subjects of his
satire. Lord Dapper incarnates for him the empty-headed beau of
Georgian London. He ridicules as well the feather-brained ladies
who by day flocked to the auction-rooms of Christopher Cock and by
night thronged the opera to applaud the great Farinelli. [22] In the
scenes of theatrical satire Fielding centered his attention on the
Cibber family. [23] Colley Cibber, whose daughter Charlotte Charke
was a member of Fielding's company, had recently so "improved"
Shakespeare's *King John* that it had been withdrawn during re-
hearsals. Theophilus, his obnoxious son, was playing his usual Pistol
role both on and off stage. Even the more reticent Susanna, Theophilus' wife, had recently attracted attention, for she and the acid-
tongued Kitty Clive, the rival queens of Drury Lane, were feuding
bitterly as to which one would play Polly in the still hugely popular
Beggar's Opera.

These topics and personalities were hardly fresh ones for the author.

[19] Egmont, *Diary*, II, 390. See Charles B. Woods, "Notes on Three of
Fielding's Plays," *PMLA*, LII (1937), 359–373.

[20] *The Daily Advertiser*, March 21, 1737, quoted in Scouten, *The London
Stage, Part 3*, II, 651.

[21] "An Adventurer in Politics" in *The Daily Gazetteer*, May 7, 1737,
indignantly takes Fielding to task for "want of intelligence of the affairs of
other nations."

[22] See Charles W. Nichols, "Social Satire in *Pasquin* and *The Historical
Register*," *Philological Quarterly*, III (1924), 309–317.

[23] See Charles W. Nichols, "Fielding and the Cibbers," *Philological
Quarterly*, I (1922), 278–289.

He had made fun of auctions and the *castrati* before, and there was always an open season on the Cibber family. What excited attention in *The Historical Register* was the pungency and daring of the political satire.

As a setting for this satire he chose the island of Corsica. The choice was not a capricious but a calculated one. Among the most discussed topics of the day was the sensational career of Baron Neuhoff, the international adventurer.[24] Reputedly Swedish-born, he had gravitated mysteriously from one European capital to another before receiving an unlikely appointment by the Sultan of Turkey as his ambassador to Morocco. In 1736 he had capped his astonishing career by turning up in Corsica as the leader of a group of island patriots fighting for independence from Genoese rule. Soon afterward he appointed himself their king and assumed the title of Theodore I. Hunted by the Genoese authorities and denounced by them as an impostor, the Baron coolly observed: "Since the Genoese have attempted to make me pass for a mountebank, I hope soon to demonstrate what conjurers they are, and set up my stage in the middle of the city of Bastia."[25]

The man was evidently a heroic charlatan, a worthy avatar of the Great Man, and it is easy to see why such a figure appealed to Fielding's imagination. It is also easy to see why the Corsican setting was apt for his purposes. Like Great Britain it was a small island, struggling to free itself from the burden of heavy taxes and a notoriously corrupt set of officials. That Fielding was not alone in sensing these analogies is evident from a contemporary essay in *Common Sense* which begins: "If I were a Corsican I should certainly be a rebel, that is, I should hazard my life and estate to recover my liberty."[26]

Using this island setting, Fielding evoked the mood of England in 1736, a year marked by violence. In Scotland discontent had blazed up in the Porteous riots. In London the militia had fired upon rebellious mobs.[27] So widespread was the disaffection that Parliament had roused itself from its usual torpor. After much deliberation it had passed a bill designed to abolish bribery and corruption. In a further

---

[24] For an account of Neuhoff see *The London Magazine*, V (1736), 282, and *The Gentleman's Magazine*, VI (1736), 490, 623.

[25] *The Gentleman's Magazine* (1736), 358. Bastia was the site of the Genoese governmental headquarters in Corsica.

[26] *Common Sense*, May 28, 1737.

[27] For an account of the riots see *The Gentleman's Magazine* (1736), 422, 474.

gesture of conciliation it had solemnly investigated the disputed election of sixteen Scottish members of Parliament all of whom, it was alleged, were of "the Ministerial complexion." [28] But such actions were ceremonious rather than meaningful. Bribery and corruption went on unabated, and the sixteen Scots retained their seats.

At the center of this web of politics was one man—Sir Robert Walpole. Evidently Fielding was both attracted and repelled by him, and in the course of his dramatic career he alluded to him again and again.[29] Sometimes the allusions are oblique, such as those in *The Author's Farce* and *Tom Thumb*. In other instances they are specific, as in *The Welsh Opera* (1731), which has been likened to "a dramatization of Lord Hervey's *Memoirs*." [30]

Like most effective satirists, Fielding was unpredictable. Though ordinarily critical of Walpole, he was independent-minded enough to satirize the opposition as well, and on one occasion he saw fit to dedicate a play to the Prime Minister, though so dark and sardonic is the tone of that comedy, *The Modern Husband* (1732), that the compliment is a dubious one.

When Walpole, the Great Man, appears in Fielding it is sometimes as a politician, sometimes as a theatrical manager, Harlequin, fiddler, or puppet-master. The notion of simultaneously satirizing two victims by superimposing one upon another is a favorite device of Fielding's.[31] It is difficult, consequently, to read his dramatic satires as consistent *pièces à clef*. Fielding preferred indirection. Certain analogies he found particularly useful, chief among them the likenesses between the world of politics and the world of the theater. To take an obvious example: he found John Rich, the famous Harlequin and manager of Covent Garden, as adroit a manipulator as Robert Walpole.

> You wonder, perhaps, at the tricks of the stage,
> Or that pantomime miracles take with the age;
> But if you examine Court, Country, and Town,
> There's nothing but Harlequin feats will go down.[32]

[28] *The Historical Register*, XXI (1736), 141.
[29] See Sheridan Baker, "Political Allusions in Fielding's *Author's Farce, Mock Doctor*, and *Tumble-down Dick*," *PMLA*, LXXVII (1962), 221–231.
[30] John Loftis, *Politics of Drama in Augustan England* (Oxford, 1963), p. 105.
[31] Baker, "Political Allusions," pp. 221–231.
[32] First quatrain of the concluding chorus in Fielding's *Tumble-down Dick* (1736).

The Historical Register is marked by this deliberate ambiguity. The bastard son of Apollo is almost certainly both Theophilus Cibber and Robert Walpole—and quite possibly Charles Fleetwood, the patentee of Drury Lane, as well. The levee scene in *Eurydice Hissed* has equal applicability to court and theater, and in the character of Pillage Fielding laughs both at his own failure with *Eurydice* and Walpole's loss of prestige after the rejection of the Excise Bill.[33]

But if Fielding's satire was often ambiguous, Walpole's reaction to it was not. Ever since *The Beggar's Opera* (1728) he had been the target of the satirists. The resounding triumph of Gay's ballad opera had made its prohibition impossible, but Walpole had contrived to suppress the performance of its successor, *Polly*. The failure of the Excise Bill had provoked a new wave of pasquinades and satires, and playgoing must often have been an uncomfortable experience for the Prime Minister.

For thirty-five nights *The Historical Register* played to packed houses. It was last performed on May 23, at which time two new plays were announced for immediate production: *Macheath Turned Pirate* (an alteration of Gay's *Polly*) and *The King and Titi*. Neither of them, it would appear, was ever acted, nor did the Great Mogul's Company perform again. Opposition politicians and journalists in the spring of 1737 had expected the imminent fall of the Ministry, but they had underestimated Walpole, and the expected revolution took place not in the world of politics but in the world of the theater.

The success of *The Historical Register* had prompted a number of attacks, notably an anonymous essay in the pro-Walpole *Daily Gazetteer*.[34] The charges brought against Fielding were numerous: that in *Pasquin* he had exposed his victims with impartial wit and humor, but that in *The Historical Register* and *Eurydice Hissed* he had descended to personal attacks; and that he and other dramatists had compared government to a farce. A true patriot, the essayist wrote, would try to hide his country's weakness rather than expose it. "The stage has a large field in the follies, vices, and passions of mankind," he concluded. "It has nothing to do with politics or religion." Fielding in his rebuttal rejected these charges.[35] He denied that he had ridi-

33 Woods, "Notes," pp. 371–373.

34 This essay by "An Adventurer in Politics" which appeared on May 7, 1737, is reprinted in John Loftis, ed., *Essays on the Theatre from Eighteenth-Century Periodicals* (Augustan Reprint Society, 1960), 54–57.

35 *Common Sense*, May 21, 1737.

–xvi–

culed either true patriotism or the party in power. He recalled Aristophanes' services to the Athenian state and the dramatist's sacred obligation to expose corruption. But his protestations did not end the controversy, and the sniping continued both in the Ministerial and Opposition papers.[36]

To view these attacks as personal, dictated by Walpole's resentment, is to misread the situation. Throughout the early 1730's the stage had increasingly come under criticism from a number of directions and for a number of reasons. Typical of the theatrical dilettantes who deplored the current state of the stage was William Popple, co-author with Aaron Hill of *The Prompter* (1734–1736). Popple's contributions to that periodical are, for the most part, laments on the decline of taste and trumpet-calls to reform.[37] The Muses of Comedy and Tragedy had abdicated, driven out by squeaking *castrati* and capering Harlequins. Sweeping changes were urgently required to bring the theater once more under the control of men of taste. Charles Fleetwood and John Rich, the patentees of Drury Lane and Covent Garden, heartily agreed to the desirability of reform—but for entirely different reasons. They had observed with apprehension the increasing popularity of non-patent theaters such as Goodman's Fields and the Little Theatre in the Haymarket and were anxious to see their own patent rights protected and their competitors forced to withdraw.

There was also parliamentary agitation to bring about some control of the theaters. Such action had been initiated in 1735, under the sponsorship of Sir John Barnard.[38] It had been nearly forty years since Jeremy Collier had fulminated against the profanity and immorality of the stage. A few half-hearted attempts had subsequently been made to regulate the theaters and actors, but many sober-minded Londoners felt that the need still existed to take action against the devil's domiciles. All this played directly into Walpole's hands.

A libellous farce, *The Golden Rump* (written, so a contemporary

---

[36] An interesting selection of these essays appears both in *The London Magazine* and *The Gentleman's Magazine* for June, 1737.

[37] See *The Prompter*, ed. William W. Appleton and Kalman Burnim (New York, 1966), *passim*.

[38] For a discussion of the Licensing Act and the events leading up to it see Watson Nicholson, *The Struggle for a Free Stage in London* (London, 1906), Ch. III.

2

suggested, at the instigation of the Prime Minister himself),[39] gave him the excuse he was looking for. On May 20, 1737, an amendment was proposed to an act of 1713 designed to bring both plays and players under the control of the Lord Chamberlain. It had its first reading on June 2 and, despite the eloquent opposition of Chesterfield and Pulteney, its final enactment on the twenty-first of that month. In essence, it limited the number of theaters to those with patents and required that all new plays and all alterations of or additions to old plays be licensed by the Lord Chamberlain.[40]

Fielding can hardly be said to be primarily responsible for this legislation which had so crippling an effect on the theater. He had no real notion, it seems, that *The Historical Register* might lead to such consequences, though at the conclusion of his Dedication to the Public he hints darkly that he intends to make use of his satiric talents "while the liberty of the press and stage subsists." After the passage of the Licensing Act Fielding realized that his career as a dramatist had come to an end, and from then on he channeled his energies into the novel. There can be no question that the loss of his talents to the theater was more than compensated for by his contributions to the novel. But his plays have been unduly neglected. Fielding's topicality, it is true, occasionally makes them difficult, but much of the satire in his plays is still valid, and his wit still flashes. To use the words of his first editor, his plays are "worthy of being preserved, being the works of a genius, who in his wildest and most inaccurate productions, yet occasionally displays the talents of a master."[41]

WILLIAM W. APPLETON

Columbia University

[39] *Apology for T[heophilus] C[ibber]* (1740), p. 94.
[40] See P. J. Crean, "The Stage Licensing Act of 1737," *Modern Philology*, XXXV (1938), 239-255.
[41] Murphy, ed., *Works*, I, 11.

THE HISTORICAL REGISTER
FOR THE YEAR 1736

Preface to the Dedication

As no man hath a more stern and inflexible hatred to flattery than myself, it hath been usual with me to send most of my performances into the world without the ornament of those epistolary prefaces commonly called dedications, a custom, however, highly censured by my bookseller, who 5 affirms it a most unchristian practice. A patron is, says he, a kind of godfather to a book, and a good author ought as carefully to provide a patron to his works as a good parent should a godfather to his children. He carries this very far and draws several resemblances between those two offices 10 (for having, in the course of his trade with dramatic writers, purchased, at a moderate computation, the fee simple of one hundred thousand similes, he is perhaps the most expert in their application, and most capable of showing likenesses, in things utterly unlike, of any man living). What, 15 says he, does more service to a book or raises curiosity in the reader equal with "dedicated to his Grace the Duke of —— or the Right Honorable the Earl of ——" in an advertisement? I think the patron here may properly be said *to give a name* to the book, and if he gives a present also, what doth 20 he less than a godfather? Which present if the author applies to his own use, what doth he other than the parent? He proceeds to show how a bookseller is a kind of dry nurse to our works, with other instances which I shall omit, having already said enough to prove the exact analogy between 25 children and books, and of the method of providing for each, which, I think, affords a sufficient precedent for throwing the following piece on the public, it having been usual for several very prudent parents to act by their children in the same manner. 30

16–17. the reader] *A–F*; a reader   24. instances] *A–F*; instance *Ap.* *Ap.*

---

12. *the fee simple*] absolute possession (*OED*).

Dedication to the Public

I hope you will pardon the presumption of this dedication, since I really did not know in what manner to apply for your leave, and since I expect no present in return (the reason, I conceive, which first introduced the ceremony of asking leave among dedicators). For surely it is somewhat absurd 5 to ask a man leave to flatter him, and he must be a very impudent or simple fellow, or both, who will give it. Asking leave to dedicate, therefore, is asking whether you will pay for your dedication, and in that sense I believe it understood by both authors and patrons. 10

But farther, the very candid reception which you have given these pieces pleads my excuse. The least civility to an author or his works hath been held, time immemorial, a just title to a dedication, which is perhaps no more than an honest return of flattery, and in this light I am certain no 15 one ever had so great (I may call it) an obligation as myself, seeing that you have honored this my performance with your presence every night of its exhibition, where you have never failed showing the greatest delight and approbation; nor am I less obliged to you for those elogiums which 20 you have been heard in all places to—but hold, I am afraid this is an ingenious way which authors have discovered to convey inward flattery to themselves, while outwardly they address it to their patron. Wherefore I shall be silent on this head, having more reasons to give why I chose you to 25 patronize these pieces: and

First, the design with which they are writ, for though all dramatic entertainments are properly calculated for the public, yet these, I may affirm, more particularly belong to you, and your diversion is not merely intended by them, 30 their design being to convey some hints which may, if you please, be of infinite service in the present state of that theatrical world whereof they treat, and which is, I think, at present so far from flourishing as one could wish, that I have with concern observed some steps lately taken, and 35

35. with concern] *A–F*; with much
concern *Ap*.

others too justly apprehended, that may much endanger
the constitution of the British Theatre. For though Mr. ——
be a very worthy man, and my very good friend, I cannot
help thinking his manner of proceeding somewhat too
arbitrary, and his method of buying actors at exorbitant   40
prices to be of very ill consequence. For the town must
reimburse him these expenses, on which account those
advanced prices so much complained of must be always
continued; which, though the people in their present
flourishing state of trade and riches may very well pay, yet   45
in worse times (if such can be supposed) I am afraid they
may fall too heavy, the consequence of which I need not
mention. Moreover, should any great genius produce a piece
of most exquisite contrivance, and which would be highly
relished by the public, though perhaps not agreeable to his   50
own taste or private interest, if he should buy off the chief
actors, such play, however excellent, must be unavoidably
sunk, and the public lose all the benefit thereof. Not to
trouble the reader with more inconveniences arising from this
argumentum argentarium, many of which are obvious enough,   55
I shall only observe that corruption hath the same influence
on all societies, all bodies, which it hath on corporeal bodies,
where we see it always produce an entire destruction and
total change. For which reason, whoever attempteth to
introduce corruption into any community doth much the   60
same thing, and ought to be treated in much the same
manner with him who poisoneth a fountain, in order to dis-
perse a contagion, which he is sure everyone will drink of.

The last excuse I shall make for this presumption is the
necessity I have of so potent a patron to defend me from the   65
iniquitous surmises of a certain anonymous dialogous author
who, in the *Gazetteer* of the 17th instant, has represented
The Historical Register as aiming, in conjunction with *The*

---

37. *Mr.* ——] Charles Fleetwood, patentee of Drury Lane.
43. *advanced prices*] Prices were raised for the pantomimes. See also
Eurydice Hissed, ll. 195–205, and notes.
55. *argumentum argentarium*] question of money.
66. *anonymous . . . author*] perhaps Lord Hervey.
67. *17th instant*] The letter actually appeared on May 7, 1737.

Miller of Mansfield, the overthrow of the M——y. If this
suggestion had been inserted in *The Craftsman* or *Common* 70
Sense, or any of those papers which nobody reads, it might
have passed unanswered, but as it appears in a paper of so general a reception as *The Gazetteer,* which lies in the window of
almost every post-house in England, it behooves me, I think,
in the most serious manner, to vindicate myself from asper- 75
tions of so evil a tendency to my future prospects. And here I
must observe that had not mankind been either very blind or
very dishonest, I need not have publicly informed them that
The Register is a ministerial pamphlet, calculated to infuse
into the minds of the people a great opinion of their ministry, 80
and thereby procure an employment for the author, who
has been often promised one, whenever he would write on
that side.

And first, can anything be plainer than the first stanza of
the Ode? 85

> This is a day, in days of yore,
> Our fathers never saw before;
> This is a day, 'tis one to ten,
> Our sons will never see again.

Plainly intimating that such times as these never were seen 90
before, nor will ever be seen again; for which the present
age are certainly obliged to their ministry.

What can be meant by the scene of politicians but to
ridicule the absurd and inadequate notions persons among
us, who have not the honor to know 'em, have of the 95
ministry and their measures? Nay, I have put some sentiments into the mouths of these characters which I was a
little apprehensive were too low even for a conversation at
an alehouse. I hope *The Gazetteer* will not find any resemblance here, as I hope he will not make such a compliment 100

---

69. *Miller of Mansfield*] Robert Dodsley's afterpiece was first performed
at Drury Lane on January 29, 1737.

70–71. *Craftsman or Common Sense*] anti-Walpole papers.

73. *The Gazetteer*] *The Daily Gazetteer* was the most important of the pro-
Walpole papers.

86. *a day*] "For *day,* in the first and third line, you may read *man,* if you
please." [Fielding's note.]

to any M——y as to suppose that such persons have been ever capable of the assurance of aiming at being at the head of a great people, or to any nation, as to suspect 'em contentedly living under such an administration.

The eagerness which these gentlemen express at applying 105 all manner of evil characters to their patrons brings to my mind a story I have somewhere read. As two gentlemen were walking the street together, the one said to the other, upon spying the figure of an ass hung out, "Bob! Bob! Look yonder! Some impudent rascal has hung out your 110 picture on a signpost." The grave companion, who had the misfortune to be extremely short-sighted, fell into a violent rage, and calling for the master of the house, threatened to prosecute him for exposing his features in that public manner. The poor landlord, as you may well conceive, was 115 extremely astonished and denied the fact, upon which the witty spark, who had just mentioned the resemblance, appeals to the mob now assembled together, who soon smoked the jest and agreed with him that the sign was the exact picture of the gentleman. At last, a good-natured man, 120 taking compassion of the poor figure whom he saw the jest of the multitude, whispered in his ear, "Sir, I see your eyes are bad and that your friend is a rascal and imposes on you. The sign hung out is the sign of an ass, nor will your picture be here unless you draw it yourself." 125

But I ask pardon for troubling the reader with an impertinent story, which can be applied only in the above-mentioned instance to my present subject.

I proceed in my defense to the scene of the Patriots, a scene which I thought would have made my fortune, seeing 130 that the favorite scheme of turning patriotism into a jest is so industriously pursued, and I will challenge all the ministerial advocates to show me, in the whole bundle of their writings, one passage where false patriotism (for I suppose they have not the impudence to mean any other) is set in a 135 more contemptible and odious light than in the aforesaid scene. I hope, too, it will be remarked that the politicians

---

109. *Bob! Bob!*] i.e., Robert Walpole.
129. *scene of the Patriots*] See *Historical Register*, III, 180–262.

are represented as a set of blundering blockheads rather
deserving pity than abhorrence, whereas the others are
represented as a set of cunning self-interested fellows who for 140
a little paltry bribe would give up the liberties and proper-
ties of their country. Here is the danger, here is the rock on
which our constitution must, if it ever does, split. The
liberties of a people have been subdued by the conquest of
valor and force, and have been betrayed by the subtle and 145
dextrous arts of refined policy; but these are rare instances,
for geniuses of this kind are not the growth of every age,
whereas if a general corruption be once introduced and
those who should be the guardians and bulwarks of our
liberty once find, or think they find, an interest in giving it 150
up, no great capacity will be required to destroy it; on the
contrary, the meanest, lowest, dirtiest fellow, if such a one
should have ever the assurance, in future ages, to mimic
power and browbeat his betters, will be as able as Machiavel
himself could have been, to root out the liberties of the 155
bravest people.

But I am aware I shall be asked who is this *Quidam* that
turns patriots into ridicule and bribes them out of their
honesty? Who but the Devil could act such a part? Is not
this the light wherein he is everywhere described in scrip- 160
ture and the writings of our best divines? Gold hath always
been his favorite bait, wherewith he fisheth for sinners, and
his laughing at the poor wretches he seduceth is as diaboli-
cal an attribute as any. Indeed it is so plain who is meant by
this *Quidam* that he who maketh any wrong application 165
thereof might as well mistake the name of Thomas for John,
or Old Nick for Old Bob.

I think I have said enough to assure every impartial
person of my innocence against all malicious insinuations;
and farther to convince them that I am a ministerial writer 170
(an honor I am highly ambitious of attaining), I shall proceed
now to obviate an opinion entertained by too many, that

---

157. *Quidam*] Walpole. See *Historical Register*, Act III, 240–262.

166. *Thomas for John*] Thomas Pelham-Holles, Duke of Newcastle, or
John, Lord Hervey, supporters of Walpole.

a certain person is sometimes the author, often the corrector
of the press, and always the patron of the *Gazetteer*. To show
the folly of this supposition I shall only insist that all persons, 175
though they should not afford him any extraordinary genius,
nor any (the least) taste in polite literature, will grant me this
datum, that the said person is a man of an ordinary capacity
and a moderate share of common sense: which, if allowed,
I think it will follow that it is impossible he should either 180
write or countenance a paper written not only without the
least glimmering of genius, the least pretension to taste, but
in direct opposition to all common sense whatever. If anyone should ask me how then is it carried on, I shall only
answer with my Politicians, "I cannot tell," unless by the 185
assistance of the old gentleman just before mentioned, who
would, I think alone protect or patronize, as I think, indeed,
he is the only person who could invent some of the schemes
avowed in that paper which, if it does not immediately
disappear, I do intend shortly to attempt conjuring it down, 190
intending to publish a paper in defense of the M——y
against the wicked, malicious, and sly insinuations conveyed
in the said paper.

You will excuse a digression so necessary to take off surmises, which may prove so prejudicial to my fortune; 195
which, however, if I should not be able to accomplish, I
hope you will make me some amends for what I suffer by
endeavoring your entertainment. The very great indulgence
you have shown my performances at the little theatre, these
two last years, have encouraged me to the proposal of a 200
subscription for carrying on that theater, for beautifying
and enlarging it and procuring a better company of actors.
If you think proper to subscribe to these proposals, I assure
you no labor shall be spared, on my side, to entertain you in
a cheaper and better manner than seems to be the intention 205

187. patronize, as] *A–F*; patronize
it, as *Ap*.

---

173. *a certain person*] perhaps Lord Hervey.
185. *I cannot tell*] See *Historical Register*, I, 167.
191. *intending . . . paper*] Fielding is, of course, being ironic.

of any other. If Nature hath given me any talents at ridiculing vice and imposture, I shall not be indolent nor afraid of exercising them while the liberty of the press and stage subsists, that is to say, while we have any liberty left among us. I am, to the public, 210

A MOST SINCERE FRIEND,
AND MOST DEVOTED SERVANT.

208–209. *while . . . subsists*] An attempt had been made in 1735 to enact legislation to control the theaters.

DRAMATIS PERSONAE

Men

MEDLEY	*Mr. Roberts*
SOURWIT	*Mr. Lacy*
LORD DAPPER	*Mr. Ward*
GROUND-IVY	*Mr. Jones*
HEN, the Auctioneer	*Mrs. Charke*
APOLLO'S BASTARD SON	*Mr. Blakes*
PISTOL	*Mr. Davis*
QUIDAM	*Mr. Smith*
	Mr. Jones
	Mr. Topping
POLITICIANS	*Mr. Woodburn*
	Mr. Smith
	Mr. Machen
	Mr. Topping
	Mr. Machen
PATRIOTS	*Mr. Pullen*
	Mr. Woodburn
BANTER	*Mr. Smith*
DANGLE	*Mr. Lowther*

Women

MRS. SCREEN	*Mrs. Haywood*
MRS. BARTER	*Miss Kawer*
	Mrs. Charke
	Mrs. Haywood
LADIES	*Mrs. Lacy*
	Miss Jones

PROMPTER, ACTORS, &c.

The Historical Register
for the Year 1736

ACT I

Scene: the Playhouse.
Enter several Players.

FIRST PLAYER.

Mr. Emphasis, good morrow! You are early at the rehearsal this morning.

EMPHASIS.

Why faith, Jack, our beer and beef sat but ill on my stomach, so I got up to try if I could not walk it off.

FIRST PLAYER.

I wish I had anything in my stomach to walk off; if matters   5 do not go better with us shortly, my teeth will forget their office.

SECOND PLAYER.

These are poor times, indeed, not like the days of *Pasquin*.

FIRST PLAYER.

Oh! name 'em not! Those were the glorious days indeed, the days of beef and punch, my friends, when come there   10 such again?

SECOND PLAYER.

Who knows what this new author may produce? Faith, I like my part very well.

FIRST PLAYER.

Nay, if variety will please the town, I am sure there is

0.1. *Scene: the Playhouse.*] *A–F; om. Ap.*

---

8. *Pasquin*] Fielding's play had had an enormously successful run at the Little Theatre in the Haymarket during the spring of 1736.

enough of it, but I could wish, methinks, the satire had 15
been a little stronger, a little plainer.

SECOND PLAYER.

Now I think it is plain enough.

FIRST PLAYER.

Hum! Ay, it is intelligible, but I would have it downright;
'gad, I fancy I could write a thing to succeed, myself.

SECOND PLAYER.

Ay, prithee, what subject wouldst thou write on? 20

FIRST PLAYER.

Why no subject at all, sir, but I would have a humming
deal of satire, and I would repeat in every page that cour-
tiers are cheats and don't pay their debts, that lawyers are
rogues, physicians blockheads, soldiers cowards, and
ministers— 25

SECOND PLAYER.

What, what, sir?

FIRST PLAYER.

Nay, I'll only name 'em, that's enough to set the audience
a-hooting.

SECOND PLAYER.

Zounds, sir, here is wit enough for a whole play in one
speech. 30

FIRST PLAYER.

For one play? Why, sir, 'tis all I have extracted out of above
a dozen.

SECOND PLAYER.

Who have we here?

FIRST PLAYER.

Some gentlemen, I suppose, come to hear the rehearsal.

Enter Sourwit *and* Lord Dapper.

LORD DAPPER.

Pray, gentlemen, don't you rehearse *The Historical Register* 35
this morning?

FIRST PLAYER.

Sir, we expect the author every minute.

SOURWIT.

What is this *Historical Register*? Is it a tragedy or a comedy?

FIRST PLAYER.

Upon my word, sir, I can't tell.

SOURWIT.

Then I suppose you have no part in it.   40

FIRST PLAYER.

Yes, sir, I have several, but—. Oh, here is the author himself.
I suppose he can tell, sir.

SOURWIT.

Faith, sir, that's more than I suppose.

Enter Medley.

MEDLEY.

My lord, your most obedient servant. This is a very great
and unexpected favor indeed, my lord. Mr. Sourwit, I kiss   45
your hands. I am very glad to see you here.

SOURWIT [*aside*].

That's more than you may be by and by, perhaps.

LORD DAPPER.

We are come to attend your rehearsal, sir. Pray, when will
it begin?

MEDLEY.

This very instant, my lord. Gentlemen, I beg you would be   50
all ready, and let the prompter bring me some copies for
these gentlemen.

SOURWIT.

Mr. Medley, you know I am a plain speaker, so you will
excuse any liberties I take.

MEDLEY.

Dear sir, you can't oblige me more.   55

SOURWIT.

Then I must tell you, sir, I am a little staggered at the name
of your piece. Doubtless, sir, you know the rules of writing,
and I can't guess how you can bring the actions of a whole
year into the circumference of four-and-twenty hours.

MEDLEY.

Sir, I have several answers to make to your objection. In the   60
first place, my piece is not of a nature confined to any rules,
as being avowedly irregular, but if it was otherwise, I think
I could quote you precedents of plays that neglect them.
Besides, sir, if I comprise the whole actions of a year in half

an hour, will you blame me or those who have done so little   65
in that time? My register is not to be filled like those of
vulgar news-writers with trash for want of news, and therefore if I say little or nothing, you may thank those who have
done little or nothing.

Enter Prompter *with books.*

Oh! Here are my books.   70

SOURWIT.

In print already, Mr. Medley?

MEDLEY.

Yes, sir, it is the safest way, for if a man stays till he is
damned, it is possible he may never get into print at all.
The town is capricious, for which reason always print as
fast as you write, that if they damn your play, they may not   75
damn your copy too.

SOURWIT.

Well, sir, and pray what is your design, your plot?

MEDLEY.

Why, sir, I have several plots, some pretty deep and some
but shallow.

SOURWIT.

I hope, sir, they all conduce to the main design.   80

MEDLEY.

Yes, sir, they do.

SOURWIT.

Pray, sir, what is that?

MEDLEY.

To divert the town and bring full houses.

SOURWIT.

Pshaw! You misunderstand me. I mean what is your moral,
your, your, your—   85

MEDLEY.

Oh, sir, I comprehend you. Why, sir, my design is to ridicule the vicious and foolish customs of the age, and that in
a fair manner, without fear, favor, or ill-nature, and without
scurrility, ill manners, or commonplace. I hope to expose
the reigning follies in such a manner that men shall laugh   90
themselves out of them before they feel that they are touched.

3

SOURWIT.

> But what thread or connection can you have in this history? For instance, how is your political connected with your theatrical?

MEDLEY.

> Oh, very easily. When my politics come to a farce, they   95
> very naturally lead to the playhouse where, let me tell you,
> there are some politicians too, where there is lying, flatter-
> ing, dissembling, promising, deceiving, and undermining, as
> well as in any court in Christendom.

Enter a Player.

PLAYER.

> Won't you begin your rehearsal, sir?   100

MEDLEY.

> Ay, ay, with all my heart. Is the music ready for the
> prologue?

SOURWIT.

> Music for the prologue!

MEDLEY.

> Ay, sir, I intend to have everything new. I had rather be
> the author of my own dulness than the publisher of other 105
> men's wit, and really, Mr. Sourwit, the subjects for pro-
> logues are utterly exhausted. I think the general method has
> been either to frighten the audience with the author's repu-
> tation, or to flatter them to give their applause, or to
> beseech them to it, and that in a manner that will serve for 110
> every play alike. Now, sir, my prologue will serve for no
> play but my own, and to that I think nothing can be better
> adapted, for as mine is the history of the year, what can be a
> properer prologue than an Ode to the New Year?

SOURWIT.

> An Ode to the New Year?   115

MEDLEY.

> Yes, sir, an Ode to the New Year. Come, begin, begin.

Enter Prompter.

---

114. *Ode to the New Year*] Colley Cibber annually composed such an ode.
See *The London Magazine*, January, 1737, p. 55.

PROMPTER.

    Sir, the prologue is ready.

SOURWIT.

    Dear Medley, let me hear you read it. Possibly it may be sung so fine I may not understand a word of it.

MEDLEY.

    Sir, you can't oblige me more.   [*Begins reading.*] 120

Ode to the New Year

This is a day in days of yore,
Our fathers never saw before:
This is a day, 'tis one to ten,
Our sons will never see again.   125
   Then sing the day,
   And sing the song,
   And thus be merry
   All day long.
This is the day,   130
And that's the night,
When the sun shall be gay,
And the moon shall be bright.
   The sun shall rise,
   All in the skies;   135
   The moon shall go,
   All down below.
   Then sing the day,
   And sing the song;
   And thus be merry   140
   All day long.

Ay, ay, come on and sing it away.

Enter singers who sing the Ode.

    There, sir, that's the very quintessence and cream of all the odes I have seen for several years last past.

SOURWIT.

    Ay, sir, I thought you would not be the publisher of another 145 man's wit?

MEDLEY.

    No more I an't, sir, for the devil of any wit did I ever see in any of them.

SOURWIT.

Oh! Your most humble servant, sir.

MEDLEY.

Yours, sir, yours. Now for my play. Prompter, are the poli-   150
ticians all ready at the table?

. PROMPTER.

I'll go and see, sir.   *Exit.*

MEDLEY.

My first scene, Mr. Sourwit, lies in the island of Corsica,
being at present the chief scene of politics of all Europe.

[Re-]enter Prompter.

PROMPTER.

Sir, they are ready.   155

MEDLEY.

Then draw the scene and discover them.

Scene draws and discovers five Politicians *sitting at a table.*

SOURWIT.

Here's a mistake in the print, Mr. Medley. I observe the
second politician is the first person who speaks.

MEDLEY.

Sir, my first and greatest politician never speaks at all. He's
a very deep man, by which, you will observe, I convey this   160
moral, that the chief art of a politician is to keep a secret.

SOURWIT.

To keep his politics a secret, I suppose you mean.

MEDLEY [*to the* Second Politician].

Come, sir, begin.

SECOND POLITICIAN.

Is King Theodore returned yet?

THIRD POLITICIAN.

No.   165

SECOND POLITICIAN.

When will he return?

161. chief] *A–F*; first *Ap.*

---

153. *Corsica*] Corsica and Genoa were at war. See Introduction, p. xiv.
159. *first . . . politician*] Robert Walpole was noted for his secrecy.
164. *King Theodore*] i.e., Baron Neuhoff, leader of the Corsican rebels.
See Introduction, p. xiv.

THIRD POLITICIAN.

I cannot tell.

SOURWIT.

This politician seems to me to know very little of the matter.

MEDLEY.

Zounds, sir! Would you have him a prophet as well as a 170 politician? You see, sir, he knows what's past, and that's all he ought to know. 'Sblood, sir, would it be in the character of a politician to make him a conjurer? Go on, gentlemen. Pray, sir [to Sourwit], don't interrupt their debates, for they are of great consequence.   175

SECOND POLITICIAN.

These mighty preparations of the Turks are certainly designed against some place or other. Now the question is, what place are they designed against? And that is a question which I cannot answer.

THIRD POLITICIAN.

But it behooves us to be upon our guard.   180

FOURTH POLITICIAN.

It does, and the reason is because we know nothing of the matter.

SECOND POLITICIAN.

You say right. It is easy for a man to guard against dangers which he knows of, but to guard against dangers which nobody knows of requires a very great politician.   185

MEDLEY [to Sourwit].

Now, sir, I suppose you think that nobody knows anything.

SOURWIT.

Faith, sir, it appears so.

MEDLEY.

Ay, sir, but there is one who knows, that little gentleman, yonder in the chair, who says nothing, knows it all.

SOURWIT.

But how do you intend to convey this knowledge to the 190 audience?

---

176. *mighty . . . Turks*] Mahmud I, Sultan of Turkey, concluded a peace with Persia in 1736 but was at war with Russia and threatened by Austria.

MEDLEY.

> Sir, they can read it in his looks. 'Sblood, sir, must not a politician be thought a wise man without his giving instances of his wisdom?

FIFTH POLITICIAN.

> Hang foreign affairs, let us apply ourselves to money.   195

OMNES.

> Ay, ay, ay.

MEDLEY.

> Gentlemen, that over again—and be sure to snatch hastily at the money. You're pretty politicians, truly.

FIFTH POLITICIAN.

> Hang foreign affairs, let us apply ourselves to money.

OMNES.

> Ay, ay, ay.   200

SECOND POLITICIAN.

> All we have to consider relating to money is how we shall get it.

THIRD POLITICIAN.

> I think we ought first to consider whether there is any to be got, which if there be, I do readily agree that the next question is—how to come at it?   205

OMNES.

> Hum.

SOURWIT.

> Pray, sir, what are these gentlemen in Corsica?

MEDLEY.

> Why, sir, they are the ablest heads in the kingdom, and consequently the greatest men, for you may be sure all well-regulated governments, as I represent this of Corsica to be, 210 will employ in their greatest posts men of the greatest capacity.

SECOND POLITICIAN.

> I have considered the matter and I find it must be by a tax.

THIRD POLITICIAN.

> I thought of that and was considering what was not taxed already.   215

---

213. *a tax*] probably an allusion either to the Excise Bill of 1733 or the Gin Bill of 1736.

SECOND POLITICIAN.

Learning. Suppose we put a tax upon Learning.

THIRD POLITICIAN.

Learning, it is true, is a useless commodity, but I think we had better lay it on Ignorance, for Learning being the property but of a very few, and those poor ones too, I am afraid we can get little among them, whereas Ignorance 220 will take in most of the great fortunes in the kingdom.

OMNES.

Ay, ay, ay.   *Exeunt* Politicians.

SOURWIT.

Faith, 'tis very generous in these gentlemen to tax themselves so readily.

MEDLEY.

Ay, and very wise too, to prevent the people's grumbling, 225 and they will have it all among themselves.

SOURWIT.

But what is become of the politicians?

MEDLEY.

They are gone, sir, they're gone. They have finished the business they met about, which was to agree on a tax. That being done, they are gone to raise it, and this, sir, is the full 230 account of the whole history of Europe, as far as we know of it, comprised in one scene.

SOURWIT.

The devil it is! Why you have not mentioned one word of France, or Spain, or the Emperor!

MEDLEY.

No, sir, I turn those over to the next year, by which time we 235 may possibly know something what they are about. At present our advices are so very uncertain I know not what to depend on. But come, sir, now you shall have a council of ladies.

SOURWIT.

Does this scene lie in Corsica too?

MEDLEY.

No, no, this lies in London. You know, sir, it would not have 240

---

234. *France ... Emperor*] France and Spain had been allied during the War of the Polish Succession (1733–1735) against Charles VI, Emperor of Austria.

been quite so proper to have brought English politicians (of
the male kind, I mean) on the stage, because our politics are
not quite so famous. But in female politicians, to the honor of
my countrywomen I say it, I believe no country can excel us.
Come, draw the scene and discover the ladies.   245

PROMPTER.

Sir, they are not here. One of them is practicing above the
stairs with a dancing-master, and I can't get her down.

MEDLEY.

I'll fetch 'em, I warrant you.   *Exit.*

SOURWIT.

Well, my lord, what does your lordship think of what you
have seen?   250

LORD DAPPER.

Faith, sir, I did not observe it, but it's damned stuff, I am
sure.

SOURWIT.

I think so, and I hope your lordship will not encourage it.
They are such men as your lordship who must reform the
age. If persons of your exquisite and refined taste will give 255
a sanction to politer entertainments, the town will soon be
ashamed of laughing at what they do now.

LORD DAPPER [*gazing around the theater*].

Really, this is a very bad house.

SOURWIT.

It is not indeed so large as the others, but I think one hears
better in it.   260

LORD DAPPER.

Pox of hearing—one can't see! One's self, I mean. Here are
no looking glasses. I love Lincoln's Inn Fields, for that
reason, better than any house in town.

SOURWIT.

Very true, my lord, but I wish your lordship would think it
worthy your consideration, as the morals of a people depend 265

251. it's] *A–F*; 'tis *Ap.*

255–257. *If . . . now*] Fielding is satirizing the type of criticism found in
Aaron Hill and William Popple's *The Prompter* (1734–1736).

262. *Lincoln's Inn Fields*] a theater currently being used by Henry Giffard's
company.

(as has been so often and well-proved) entirely on their
public diversions, it would be of great consequence that
those of the sublimest kind should meet with your lordship's
and the rest of the nobility's countenance.

LORD DAPPER.

Mr. Sourwit, I am always ready to give my countenance to   270
anything of that kind which might bring the best company
together, for as one does not go to see the play, but the
company, I think that's chiefly to be considered, and therefore I am always ready to countenance good plays.

SOURWIT.

No one is a better judge what is so than your lordship.   275

LORD DAPPER.

Not I indeed, Mr. Sourwit, but as I am one half of the play
in the Green Room, talking to the actresses, and the other
half in the boxes, talking to the women of quality, I have an
opportunity of seeing something of the play, and perhaps
may be as good a judge as another.   280

Enter Medley.

MEDLEY.

My lord, the ladies cannot begin yet. If your lordship will
honor me in the Green Room, where you will find it
pleasanter than upon this cold stage—

LORD DAPPER.

With all my heart. —Come, Mr. Sourwit.

SOURWIT.

I attend your lordship.   *Exeunt.* 285

PROMPTER.

Thou art a sweet judge of plays, indeed, and yet it is in the
power of such sparks as these to damn an honest fellow both
in his profit and reputation.   *Exit.*

270–280. *I am ... as another*] Cf. Lord Dapper's views to those expressed
in James Ralph, *The Taste of the Town* (1731), Essay 5.
277. *the Green Room*] backstage reception room.

ACT II

[*The Playhouse.*]
Enter Medley, Lord Dapper, Sourwit, *and* Prompter.

MEDLEY.

Come, draw the scene and discover the ladies in council.—
[*To* Lord Dapper.] Pray, my lord, sit.

The scene draws and discovers four Ladies.

SOURWIT.

What are these ladies assembled about?

MEDLEY.

Affaires of great importance, as you will see. —Please to
begin, all of you.   5

The Ladies *all speak together.*

ALL LADIES.

Was you at the Opera, madam, last night?

SECOND LADY.

Who can miss an opera while Farinello stays?

THIRD LADY.

Sure he is the charmingest creature!

FOURTH LADY.

He's everything in the world one could wish!

FIRST LADY.

Almost everything one could wish!   10

SECOND LADY.

They say there's a lady in the city has a child by him.

ALL LADIES.

Ha, ha, ha!

FIRST LADY.

Well, it must be charming to have a child by him.

THIRD LADY.

Madam, I met a lady in a visit the other day with three!

---

1. *draw the scene*] i.e., pull open the shutters which conceal the rear stage.
7. *Farinello*] Carlo Broschi (1705–1782), the most celebrated of the *castrati.*
11. *They . . . him*] Humorous verses to this effect were common during the period.

ALL LADIES.

    All Farinellos?   15

THIRD LADY.

    All Farinellos, all in wax.

FIRST LADY.

    Oh Gemini! Who makes them? I'll send and bespeak half a
dozen tomorrow morning.

SECOND LADY.

    I'll have as many as I can cram into a coach with me.

SOURWIT.

    Mr. Medley, sir, is this history? This must be invention.   20

MEDLEY.

    Upon my word, sir, 'tis fact, and I take it to be the most
extraordinary accident that has happened in the whole
year, and as well worth recording. Faith, sir, let me tell you,
I take it to be ominous, for if we go on to improve in luxury,
effeminacy, and debauchery, as we have done lately, the   25
next age, for ought I know, may be more like the children
of squeaking Italians than hardy Britons.

ALL LADIES.

    Don't interrupt us, dear sir.

FIRST LADY.

    What mighty pretty company they must be!

SECOND LADY.

    Oh, the prettiest company in the world!   30

THIRD LADY.

    If one could but teach them to sing like their father.

FOURTH LADY.

    I'm afraid my husband won't let me keep them, for he hates
I should be fond of anything but himself.

ALL LADIES.

    Oh, the unreasonable creature!

FIRST LADY.

    If my husband was to make any objection to my having 'em,   35
I'd run away from him and take the dear babies with me.

---

16. *all in wax*] an allusion to the vogue for wax figures, which were sold
at the New Exchange.

26–27. *more . . . Britons*] Cf. *The Prompter* No. 14, December 27, 1734.

36. *babies*] dolls.

MEDLEY.

    Come, enter Beau Dangle.

Enter Dangle.

DANGLE.

    Fie upon it, ladies! What are you doing here? Why are not
you at the auction? Mr. Hen has been in the pulpit this half
hour.   40

FIRST LADY.

    Oh, dear Mr. Hen! I ask his pardon. I never miss him.

SECOND LADY.

    What's to be sold today?

FIRST LADY.

    Oh, I never mind that. There will be all the world there.

DANGLE.

    You'll find it almost impossible to get in.

ALL LADIES.

    Oh, I shall be quite miserable if I don't get in.   45

DANGLE.

    Then you must not lose a moment.

ALL LADIES.

    Oh, not a moment for the world!   *Exeunt* Ladies.

MEDLEY.

    There—they are gone.

SOURWIT.

    I am glad on't with all my heart.

LORD DAPPER.

    Upon my word, Mr. Medley, that last is an exceeding good   50
scene, and full of a great deal of politeness, good sense, and
philosophy.

MEDLEY.

    It's Nature, my lord, it's Nature.

SOURWIT.

    Faith, sir, the ladies are much obliged to you.

MEDLEY.

    Faith, sir, it's more than I desire such ladies, as I represent   55

53. It's . . . it's] *A–F*; 'Tis . . . 'tis   55. it's] *A–F*; 'tis *Ap.*
Ap.

---

    39. *Mr. Hen*] Christopher Cock, a celebrated auctioneer.
    39. *pulpit*] an auctioneer's desk or platform (*OED*).

here, should be. As for the nobler part of the sex, for whom
I have the greatest honor, their characters can be no better
set off than by ridiculing that light, trifling, giddy-headed
crew who are a scandal to their own sex and a curse on ours.

PROMPTER.

Gentlemen, you must make room, for the curtain must be   60
let down to prepare the auction room.

MEDLEY [*to* Lord Dapper].

My lord, I believe you will be best before the curtain for
we have but little room behind and a great deal to do.

[*They move to the front of the stage. The curtain descends.*]

SOURWIT.

Upon my word, Mr. Medley, I must ask you the same
question which one of your ladies did just now. What do you   65
intend to sell at this auction? The whole stock-in-trade of
some milliner or mercer who has left off business?

MEDLEY.

Sir, I intend to sell such things as was never sold in any
auction before, nor ever will again. I can assure you, Mr.
Sourwit, this scene, which I look on as the best in the whole   70
performance, will require a very deep attention. Sir, if you
should take one pinch of snuff during the whole scene, you
will lose a joke by it, and yet they lie pretty deep too, and
may escape observation from a moderate understanding
unless very closely attended to.   75

SOURWIT.

I hope, however, they don't lie as deep as the dumb gentleman's politics did in the first act. If so, nothing but an
inspired understanding can come at 'em.

MEDLEY.

Sir, this scene is writ in allegory, and though I have en-
deavored to make it as plain as possible, yet all allegory will   80
require a strict attention to be understood, sir.

PROMPTER.

Sir, everything is ready.

MEDLEY.

Then draw up the curtain. —Come, enter Mrs. Screen and
Mrs. Barter.   [*The curtain is drawn up.*]

The Auction.

Scene an auction room, a pulpit and forms placed, and several people walking about, some seated near the pulpit. Enter Mrs. Screen *and* Mrs. Barter.

MRS. SCREEN.

Dear Mrs. Barter!   85

MRS. BARTER.

Dear madam! You are early today.

MRS. SCREEN.

Oh, if one does not get near the pulpit one does nothing, and
I intend to buy a great deal today. I believe I shall buy the
whole auction, at least if things go cheap. You won't bid
against me?   90

MRS. BARTER.

You know I never bid for anything.

Enter Banter *and* Dangle.

BANTER.

That's true, Mrs. Barter. I'll be your evidence.

MRS. SCREEN.

Are you come? Now I suppose we shall have fine bidding.
I don't expect to buy cheaper than at a shop.

BANTER.

That's unkind, Mrs. Screen. You know I never bid against   95
you. It would be cruel to bid against a lady who frequents
auctions, only with a design one day or other to make one
great auction of her own. No, no, I will not prevent the
filling your warehouse. I assure you, I bid against no haber-
dashers of all wares.   100

MRS. BARTER.

You are a mighty civil person, truly.

BANTER.

You need not take up the cudgels, madam, who are of no
more consequence at an auction than a mayor at a sessions.
You only come here where you have nothing to do to show
people you have nothing to do anywhere else.   105

MRS. BARTER.

I don't come to say rude things to all the world, as
you do.

84.2. *forms*] benches (*OED*).

BANTER.

No, the world may thank heaven that did not give you wit
enough to do that.

MRS. SCREEN.

Let him alone. He will have his jest.   110

MRS. BARTER.

You don't think I mind him, I hope? But pray, sir, of what
great use is your friend, Mr. Dangle, here?

BANTER.

Oh, he is of very great use to all women of understanding.

DANGLE.

Ay! Of what use am I, pray?

BANTER.

To keep 'em at home, that they may not hear the silly things 115
you say to 'em.

MRS. SCREEN.

I hope, Mr. Banter, you will not banish all people from
places where they are of no consequence; you will allow 'em
to go to an assembly, or a masquerade, without either
playing, dancing, or intriguing; you will let people go to an 120
opera without any ear, to a play without any taste, and to
church without any religion?

Enter Mr. Hen, *auctioneer, bowing.*

Oh! Dear Mr. Hen, I am glad you are come. You are
horrible late today.

HEN.

Madam, I am just mounting the pulpit. I hope you like the 125
catalogue, ladies?

MRS. SCREEN.

There are some good things here, if you are not too dilatory
with your hammer.

BANTER [*to an attendant*].

Boy, give me a catalogue.

HEN (*in the pulpit*).

I dare swear, gentlemen and ladies, this auction will give 130
general satisfaction. It is the first of its kind which I ever had
the honor to exhibit, and I believe I may challenge the
world to produce some of the curiosities which this choice
cabinet contains: a catalogue of curiosities which were col-
lected by the indefatigable pains of that celebrated virtuoso, 135

Peter Humdrum, Esquire, which will be sold by auction, by
Christopher Hen, on Monday the 21st day of March, beginning at Lot 1. Gentlemen and ladies, this is Lot 1: a most
curious remnant of political honesty. Who puts it up,
gentlemen? It will make you a very good cloak. You see   140
it's both sides alike, so you may turn it as often as you will.
Come—five pounds for this curious remnant. I assure you,
several great men have made their birthday suits out of the
same piece. It will wear forever and never be the worse for
wearing. —Five pounds is bid. Nobody more than five   145
pounds for this curious piece of political honesty? Five
pound. No more? (*Knocks.*) Lord Both-Sides. —Lot 2.
A most delicate piece of patriotism, gentlemen. Who bids?
Ten pounds for this piece of patriotism?

FIRST COURTIER.

I would not wear it for a thousand pound.   150

HEN.

Sir, I assure you several gentlemen at court have worn the
same. 'Tis a quite different thing within to what it is without.

FIRST COURTIER.

Sir, it is prohibited goods. I shan't run the risk of being
brought into Westminster Hall for wearing it.

HEN.

You take it for the old patriotism, whereas it is indeed like   155
that in nothing but the cut, but, alas! sir, there is a great
difference in the stuff. But, sir, I don't propose this for a
town suit. This is only proper for the country. Consider,
gentlemen, what a figure this will make at an election.
Come—five pound? One guinea? [*Silence.*]   Put patriot-   160
ism by.

BANTER.

Ay, put it by. One day or other it may be in fashion.

HEN.

Lot 3. Three grains of modesty. Come, ladies, consider how
scarce this valuable commodity is.

---

137. *21st day of March*] the date of the first performance of *The Historical
Register*.
143. *birthday suits*] clothes worn on the King's birthday.
154. *Westminster Hall*] the law courts.

MRS. SCREEN.

Yes, and out of fashion too, Mr. Hen.   165

HEN.

I ask your pardon, madam. It is true French, I assure you,
and never changes color on any account. Half a crown for
all this modesty? —Is there not one lady in the room who
wants any modesty?

FIRST LADY.

Pray, sir, what is it? For I can't see it at this distance.   170

HEN.

It cannot be seen at any distance, madam, but it is a
beautiful powder, which makes a fine wash for the complexion.

MRS. SCREEN.

I thought you said it was true French and would not change
the color of the skin?   175

HEN.

No, it will not, madam, but it serves mighty well to blush
behind a fan with, or to wear under a lady's mask at a masquerade. [*Silence.*] What? Nobody bid? Well, lay
modesty aside. —Lot 4. One bottle of courage, formerly in
the possession of Lieutenant-Colonel Ezekiel Pipkin, citizen,   180
alderman, and tallow-chandler. [*Silence.*] What? Is there
no officer of the trained bands here? Or it will serve an
officer of the army as well in time of peace, nay, even in
war, gentlemen; it will serve all of you who sell out.

FIRST OFFICER.

Is the bottle whole? Is there no crack in it?   185

HEN.

None, sir, I assure you, though it has been in many engage-
ments in Tothill Fields. Nay, it has served a campaign or two
in Hyde Park since the alderman's death. It will never

---

172. *wash*] a liquid cosmetic (*OED*).

182. *trained bands*] trained companies of citizen soldiery (*OED*).

184. *sell out*] i.e., sell their commissions.

187. *Tothill Fields*] a section of Westminster, the scene of riots in July,
1736. See *The Gentleman's Magazine*, 1736, pp. 422, 525.

187–188. *campaign . . . Park*] possibly an allusion to Clifford Phillips, justice of the peace, whose troops seized some of the rioters in August of 1736.

waste while you stay at home, but it evaporates immediately
if carried abroad.   190

FIRST OFFICER.

Damn me, I don't want it, but a man can't have too much
courage. Three shillings for it!

HEN.

Three shillings are bid for this bottle of courage.

FIRST BEAU.

Four!

BANTER.

What do you bid for courage for?   195

FIRST BEAU.

Not for myself, but I have a commission to buy it for a lady.

FIRST OFFICER.

Five!

HEN.

Five shillings, five shillings for all this courage. Nobody
more than five shillings?— (*Knocks.*)   Your name, sir?

FIRST OFFICER.

Macdonald O'Thunder.   200

HEN.

Lot 5 and Lot 6. All the wit lately belonging to Mr. Hugh
Pantomime, composer of entertainments for the playhouses,
and Mr. William Goosequill, composer of political papers in
defense of a ministry. Shall I put up these together?

BANTER.

Ay, it is a pity to part them. Where are they?   205

HEN.

Sir, in the next room, where any gentleman may see them,
but they are too heavy to bring in. There are near three
hundred volumes in folio.

---

190. *if carried abroad*] perhaps an allusion to Walpole's policy of non-intervention in Europe.

200. *Macdonald O'Thunder*] A soldier of fortune, one Macdonal, was drilling King Theodore of Corsica's troops. See *The Gentleman's Magazine*, 1736, p. 259.

201–202. *Hugh Pantomime*] probably John Rich of Covent Garden.

203. *William Goosequill*] probably William Arnall, one of Walpole's political hack-writers.

BANTER.

Put them by. Who the devil would bid for them unless he
was the manager of some house or other? The town has 210
paid enough for their works already.

HEN.

Lot 7. A very neat clear conscience, which has been worn
by a judge and a bishop.

MRS. SCREEN.

It is as clean as if it was new.

HEN.

Yes, no dirt will stick to it, and pray observe how capacious 215
it is. It has one particular quality—put as much as you will
into it, it is never full. Come, gentlemen, don't be afraid to
bid for this, for whoever has it will never be poor.

FIRST BEAU.

One shilling for it.

HEN.

Oh fie, sir! I am sure you want it, for if you had any con- 220
science you would put it up at more than that. Come, fifty
pound for this conscience.

BANTER.

I'll give fifty pound to get rid of my conscience with all
my heart.

HEN.

Well, gentlemen, I see you are resolved not to bid for it, so 225
I'll lay it by. —Come, Lot 8. A very considerable quantity
of interest at court. Come, a hundred pound for this interest
at court.

OMNES.

For me, Mr. Hen!

HEN.

A hundred pound is bid in a hundred places, gentlemen.   230

FIRST BEAU.

Two hundred pound!

HEN.

Two hundred pound, two hundred and fifty, three hundred

222, 223, 227. pound] *A–F*; pounds *Ap.*
Ap.   231, 232, 233. pound] *A–F*; pounds
230. pound is] *A–F*; pounds are   *Ap.*

pound, three hundred and fifty, four hundred, five hundred, six hundred, a thousand! A thousand pound is bid, gentlemen. Nobody more than a thousand pounds for this interest at court? Nobody more than one thousand? (*Knocks.*) Mr. Littlewit.

BANTER.

Damn me, I know a shop where I can buy it for less.

LORD DAPPER.

Egad, you took me in, Mr. Medley. I could not help bidding for it.

MEDLEY.

It's a sure sign it's Nature, my lord, and I should not be surprised to see the whole audience stand up and bid for it too.

HEN.

All the cardinal virtues—Lot 9. Come, gentlemen, put in these cardinal virtues.

GENTLEMAN.

Eighteen pence.

HEN.

Eighteen pence is bid for these cardinal virtues. Nobody more than eighteen pence? Eighteen pence for all these cardinal virtues? Nobody more? All these virtues, gentlemen, are going for eighteen pence. Perhaps there is not so much more virtue in the world as here is, and all going for eighteen pence. (*Knocks.*) Your name, sir?

GENTLEMAN.

Sir, here's a mistake. I thought you had said a *cardinal's* virtues. 'Sblood, sir, I thought to have bought a pennyworth. Here's temperance and chastity and a pack of stuff that I would not give three farthings for.

HEN.

Well, lay 'em by. —Lot 10 and Lot 11. A great deal of Wit and a little Common Sense.

BANTER.

Why do you put up these together? They have no relation to each other.

234. pound] *A–F; om. Ap.*   241. It's . . . it's] *A–F;* 'Tis . . . 'tis *Ap.*

HEN.

Well, the Sense by itself then —Lot 10. A little Common
Sense. I assure you, gentlemen, this is a very valuable commodity. Come, who puts it in?   [*Silence.*]

MEDLEY.

You observe, as valuable as it is, nobody bids. I take this, if
I may speak in the style of a great writer, to be a most 265
emphatical silence. You see, Mr. Sourwit, no one speaks
against this lot, and the reason nobody bids for it is because
everyone thinks he has it.

HEN.

Lay it by. I'll keep it myself. —Lot 12.   *Drum beats.*

SOURWIT.

Hey day! What's to be done now, Mr. Medley?   270

MEDLEY.

Now, sir, the sport begins.

Enter a Gentleman *laughing. Huzza within.*

BANTER.

What's the matter?

GENTLEMAN.

There's a sight without would kill all mankind with laughing. Pistol is run mad and thinks himself a Great Man,
and he's marching through the streets with a drum and 275
fiddles.

BANTER.

Please heaven, I'll go and see this sight.   *Exit.*

OMNES.

And so will I.

Exeunt. [Lord Dapper, Medley, Sourwit *and* Hen *remain.*]

HEN.

Nay, if everyone else goes, I don't know why I should stay
behind.   *Exit.* 280

LORD DAPPER.

Mr. Sourwit, we'll go too.

---

265. *style . . . writer*] probably Addison.
274. *Pistol*] Theophilus Cibber, Colley's son, was famous for his performance as Pistol in *Henry V.*

MEDLEY.

If your lordship will have but a little patience till the scene
be changed, you shall see him on the stage.

SOURWIT.

Is not this jest a little overacted?

MEDLEY.

I warrant we don't overact him half so much as he does his 285
parts, though 'tis not so much his acting capacity which I
intend to exhibit as his ministerial.

SOURWIT.

His ministerial!

MEDLEY.

Yes, sir. You may remember I told you before my rehearsal
that there was a strict resemblance between the states 290
political and theatrical. There is a ministry in the latter as
well as the former, and I believe as weak a ministry as any
poor kingdom could ever boast of. Parts are given in the
latter to actors with much the same regard to capacity as
places in the former have sometimes been, in former ages, I 295
mean. And though the public damn both, yet while they
both receive their pay, they laugh at the public behind the
scenes. And if one considers the plays that come from one
part, and the writings from the other, one would be apt to
think the same authors were retained in both. —But come, 300
change the scene into the street, and then *Enter Pistol cum
suis.* —Hitherto, Mr. Sourwit, as we have had only to do
with inferior characters such as beaux and tailors, and so
forth, we have dealt in the prosaic. Now we are going to
introduce a more considerable person, our Muse will rise in 305
her style. Now, sir, for a taste of the sublime. Come! Enter
Pistol!   *Drum beats and fiddles play.*

Enter Pistol *and Mob.*

PISTOL.

Associates, brethren, countrymen and friends,
Partakers with us in this glorious enterprise,
Which for our consort we have undertaken,   310
It grieves us much, yes, by the gods it does!

---

310. *our consort*] Susanna Cibber.

That we whose great ability and parts
Have raised us to this pinnacle of power,
Entitling us Prime Minister theatrical,
That we should with an upstart of the stage   315
Contend successless on our consort's side.
But though by just hereditary right
We claim a lawless power, yet for some reasons,
Which to ourself we keep as yet concealed,
Thus to the public deign we to appeal.   [*Kneels.*] 320
Behold how humbly the great Pistol kneels.
Say then, O town, is it your royal will
That my great consort represent the part
Of Polly Peachum in *The Beggar's Opera*?   *Mob hiss.*
Thanks to the town—that hiss speaks their assent.   325
Such was the hiss that spoke the great applause
Our mighty father met with when he brought
His *Riddle* on the stage. Such was the hiss
Welcomed his *Caesar* to the Egyptian shore;
Such was the hiss in which great *John* should have expired. 330
But wherefore do I try in vain to number
Those glorious hisses which from age to age
Our family has borne triumphant from the stage?

MEDLEY.

Get thee gone for the prettiest hero that ever was shown on
any stage.   *Exit* Pistol [*and Mob.*] 335

SOURWIT.

Short and sweet, faith. What—are we to have no more of
him?

MEDLEY.

Ay, ay, sir. He's only gone to take a little breath.

---

314. *Prime Minister theatrical*] Theophilus Cibber had been functioning as
Fleetwood's deputy-manager at Drury Lane.

315. *an . . . stage*] Kitty Clive, an established favorite, was Susanna
Cibber's rival for the role of Polly in *The Beggar's Opera*.

317. *by . . . right*] i.e., as Colley Cibber's son.

328. *Riddle*] Colley Cibber's *Love in a Riddle* (1729) had been damned.

329. *Caesar*] Colley Cibber's tragedy, *Caesar in Egypt*, produced in 1724,
had also failed.

330. *John*] Colley Cibber's alteration of *King John* had been put into
rehearsal in 1736 but was withdrawn. It was finally produced in 1745.

LORD DAPPER.

If you please, sir, in the meantime we'll go take a little fire,
for 'tis confounded cold upon the stage.   340

MEDLEY.

I wait upon your lordship. Stop the rehearsal a few
moments. We'll be back again instantly.   *Exeunt.*

ACT III

[*The Playhouse.*]
Enter Medley, Sourwit *and* Lord Dapper.

MEDLEY.

Now, my lord, for my modern Apollo. Come, make all
things ready and draw the scene as soon as you can.

SOURWIT.

Modern? Why modern? You commonplace satirists are
always endeavoring to persuade us that the age we live in
is worse than any other has been, whereas mankind have   5
differed very little since the world began, for one age has
been as bad as another.

MEDLEY.

Mr. Sourwit, I do not deny that men have been always bad
enough. Vice and folly are not the invention of our age, but
I will maintain that what I intend to ridicule in the follow-   10
ing scene is the whole and sole production and invention of
some people now living. And, faith, let me tell you, though
perhaps the public may not be the better for it, it is an
invention exceeding all the discoveries of every phil-
osopher or mathematician from the beginning of the world   15
to this day.

SOURWIT.

Ay, pray what is it?

MEDLEY.

Why, sir, it is a discovery lately found out that a man of
great parts, learning, and virtue, is fit for no employment
whatever. That an estate renders a man unfit to be trusted,   20
that being a blockhead is a qualification for business, that
honesty is the only sort of folly for which a man ought to be
utterly neglected and condemned. And—but here is the
inventor himself.

Scene draws and discovers [the Prompter, First Player, *and* the bastard
son of] Apollo *in a great chair, surrounded by attendants.*

Come, bring him forward, that the audience may see and   25
hear him. You must know, sir, this is a bastard of Apollo,

---

26. *this . . . Apollo*] This figure has been identified variously as Walpole,
Theophilus Cibber, and Charles Fleetwood, patentee of Drury Lane.

begotten on that beautiful nymph Moria, who sold oranges
to Thespis' company, or rather cartload of comedians, and
being a great favorite of his father's, the old gentleman
settled upon him the entire direction of all our playhouses   30
and poetical performances whatever.

APOLLO.

Prompter?

PROMPTER.

Sir?

APOLLO.

Is there anything to be done?

PROMPTER.

Yes, sir, this play is to be cast.   [*Holds out a script.*]   35

APOLLO.

Give it me. *The Life and Death of King John*, written by
Shakespeare. Who can act the King?

PROMPTER.

Pistol, sir. He loves to act it behind the scenes.

APOLLO [*examining the script*].

Here are a parcel of English lords.

PROMPTER.

Their parts are of little consequence. I will take care to cast   40
them.

APOLLO.

Do, but be sure you will give them to actors who will mind
their cues. *Faulconbridge.* What sort of a character is he?

PROMPTER.

Sir, he is a warrior. My cousin here will do him very well.

FIRST PLAYER.

I do a warrior! I never learned to fence!   45

APOLLO.

No matter, you will have no occasion to fight. Can you look
fierce and speak well?

FIRST PLAYER [*fiercely*].

Boh!

---

27. *Moria*] perhaps an allusion to Walpole's mistress, Maria (Molly)
Skerett.

36–37. *written by Shakespeare*] Shakespeare's version had been played at
the Little Theatre in the Haymarket on March 4, 1737, by Fielding's
troupe.

APOLLO.

I would not desire a better warrior in the house than yourself. [*Re-examines script.*]   *Robert Faulconbridge.* What is this   50
Robert?

PROMPTER

Really, sir, I don't well know what he is. His chief desire
seems to be for land, I think. He is no very considerable
character. Anybody may do him well enough, or if you
leave him quite out the play will be little the worse for it.   55

APOLLO.

Well, I leave it to you. —*Peter of Pomfret,* a prophet. Have
you anybody that looks like a prophet?

PROMPTER.

I have one that looks like a fool.

APOLLO.

He'll do. —*Philip of France.*

PROMPTER.

I have cast all the French parts except the ambassador.   60

APOLLO.

Who shall do it? His part is but short. Have you never
a good genteel figure and one that can dance? For as the
English are the politest people in Europe, it will be mighty
proper that the ambassador should be able at his arrival to
entertain them with a jig or two.   65

PROMPTER.

Truly, sir, here are abundance of dancing-masters in the
house who do little or nothing for their money.

APOLLO.

Give it to one of them. See that he has a little drollery
though in him, for Shakespeare seems to have intended him
as a ridiculous character, and only to make the audience   70
laugh.

SOURWIT.

What's that, sir? Do you affirm that Shakespeare intended
the Ambassador Chatillon a ridiculous character?

---

50. *Robert*] presumably an allusion to Walpole's given name—particularly in view of ll. 53–55.

60. *the ambassador*] Chatillon, the ambassador, and Peter of Pomfret are
omitted in the Cibber version.

72–73. *Do . . . character*] perhaps an allusion to Theodore de Chavigny,
the French ambassador, who was disliked by Walpole.

MEDLEY.

No, sir, I don't.

SOURWIT.

Oh, sir, your humble servant, then I misunderstood you. I   75
thought I had heard him say so.

MEDLEY.

Yes, sir, but I shall not stand to all he says.

SOURWIT.

But, sir, you should not put a wrong sentiment into the
mouth of the God of Wit.

MEDLEY.

I tell you, he is the God only of Modern Wit, and he has a   80
very just right to be God of most of the Modern Wits that I
know; of some who are liked for their wit; of some who are
preferred for their wit; of some who live by their wit; of
those ingenious gentlemen who damn plays, and those who
write them too, perhaps. Here comes one of his votaries.   85
Come—enter, enter! Enter Mr. Ground-Ivy.

Enter Ground-Ivy.

GROUND-IVY.

What are you doing here?

APOLLO.

I am casting the parts in the tragedy of *King John*.

GROUND-IVY.

Then you are casting the parts in a tragedy that won't do.

APOLLO.

How, sir! Was it not written by Shakespeare, and was not   90
Shakespeare one of the greatest geniuses that ever lived?

GROUND-IVY.

No, sir. Shakespeare was a pretty fellow and said some
things which only want a little of my licking to do well
enough. *King John* as now writ will not do. —But a word in
your ear. I will make him do.   95

APOLLO.

How?

---

86. *Ground-Ivy*] Colley Cibber.

GROUND-IVY.

By alteration, sir. It was a maxim of mine, when I was at the
head of theatrical affairs, that no play, though ever so good,
would do without alteration. For instance, in the play
before us the Bastard *Faulconbridge* is a most effeminate 100
character, for which reason I would cut him out and put all
his sentiments in the mouth of *Constance*, who is so much
properer to speak them. —Let me tell you, Mr. Apollo,
propriety of character, dignity of diction, and emphasis of
sentiment are things I chiefly consider on these occasions. 105

PROMPTER.

I am only afraid, as Shakespeare is so popular an author
and you, asking your pardon, so unpopular.

GROUND-IVY.

Damn me, I'll write to the town and desire them to be civil,
and that in so modest a manner that an army of Cossacks
shall be melted. I'll tell them that no actors are equal to me 110
and no authors ever were superior. And how do you think
I can insinuate that in a modest manner?

PROMPTER.

Nay, faith, I can't tell.

GROUND-IVY.

Why, I'll tell them that the former only tread on my heels,
and that the greatest among the latter have been damned 115
as well as myself; and after that, what do you think of your
popularity? I can tell you, Mr. Prompter, I have seen things
carried in the House against the voice of the people before
today.

APOLLO.

Let them hiss. Let them hiss and grumble as much as they 120
please, as long as we get their money.

MEDLEY.

There, sir, is the sentiment of a Great Man, and worthy to
come from the great Apollo himself.

97–98. *when . . . affairs*] Cibber had been active in the management of
Drury Lane from 1710 to 1732.

100–102. *the Bastard . . . Constance*] Cibber had done so in his alteration
of *King John*.

SOURWIT.

He's worthy his sire, indeed, to think of this gentleman for
altering Shakespeare.   125

MEDLEY.

Sir, I will maintain this gentleman as proper as any man in
the kingdom for the business.

SOURWIT.

Indeed!

MEDLEY.

Ay, sir, for as Shakespeare is already good enough for people
of taste, he must be altered to the palates of those who have 130
none; and if you will grant that, who can be properer to
alter him for the worse? But if you are so zealous in old
Shakespeare's cause, perhaps you may find by and by all this
come to nothing. —Now for *Pistol*.

Pistol enters and overturns his father.

GROUND-IVY.

Pox on't! The boy treads close on my heels in a literal sense. 135

PISTOL.

Your pardon, sir, why will you not obey
Your son's advice and give him still his way;
For you, and all who will oppose his force,
Must be o'erthrown in his triumphant course.

SOURWIT.

I hope, sir, your *Pistol* is not intended to burlesque Shake- 140
speare.

MEDLEY.

No, sir, I have too great an honor for Shakespeare to think
of burlesquing him, and to be sure of not burlesquing him I
will never attempt to alter him, for fear of burlesquing him
by accident, as perhaps some others have done.   145

LORD DAPPER.

Pistol is the young Captain.

MEDLEY.

My lord, *Pistol* is every insignificant fellow in town who
fancies himself of great consequence and is of none. He is my
Lord *Pistol*, Captain *Pistol*, Counsellor *Pistol*, Alderman
Pistol, Beau *Pistol*, and—and—odso, what was I going to 150
say? —Come, go on.

APOLLO.

Prompter, take care that all things go well. We will retire, my friend, and read *King John*.

> *Exeunt.* [Medley, Sourwit *and* Lord Dapper *remain.*]

SOURWIT.

To what purpose, sir, was Mr. *Pistol* introduced?

MEDLEY.

To no purpose at all, sir. It's all in character, sir, and 155
plainly shows of what mighty consequence he is. And there
ends my article from the theater.

SOURWIT.

Hey day! What's become of your two *Pollys*?

MEDLEY.

Damned, sir, damned. They were damned at my first
rehearsal, for which reason I have cut them out; and to tell 160
you the truth, I think the town has honored 'em enough
with talking of 'em for a whole month; though, faith, I
believe it was owing to their having nothing else to talk of.
—Well, now for my Patriots. You will observe, Mr. Sourwit,
that I place my Politicians and Patriots at opposite ends of 165
my piece, which I do, sir, to show the wide difference
between them. I begin with my Politicians, to signify that
they will always have the preference in the world to Patriots,
and I end with Patriots, to leave a good relish in the mouths
of my audience.   170

SOURWIT.

Ay? By your Dance of Patriots one would think you intended to turn patriotism into a jest.

MEDLEY.

So I do. But don't you observe I conclude the whole with
a Dance of Patriots, which plainly intimates that when
patriotism is turned into a jest, there is an end of the whole 175
play. Come—enter four Patriots. You observe I have not so
many Patriots as Politicians. You will collect from thence
that they are not so plenty.

---

158. *two Pollys*] Susanna Cibber and Kitty Clive.

164. *Patriots*] The word was widely and ironically used to indicate a
member of Walpole's opposition.

SOURWIT.

Where does the scene lie now, sir?

MEDLEY.

In Corsica, sir, all in Corsica.   180

Enter four Patriots *from different doors, who meet in the center and shake hands.*

SOURWIT.

These Patriots seem to equal your greatest Politicians in their silence.

MEDLEY.

Sir, what they think now cannot well be spoke, but you may conjecture a great deal from their shaking their heads. They will speak by and by, as soon as they are a little heated with 185 wine. You cannot, however, expect any great speaking in this scene, for though I do not make my Patriots Politicians, I don't make them fools.

SOURWIT.

But, methinks, your Patriots are a set of shabby fellows.

MEDLEY.

They are cheaper dressed. Besides, no man can be too low 190 for a Patriot, though perhaps it is possible he may be too high.

FIRST PATRIOT.

Prosperity to Corsica!

SECOND PATRIOT.

Liberty and Prosperity!

THIRD PATRIOT.

Success to trade!   195

FOURTH PATRIOT.

Ay, to trade—to trade—particularly to my shop!

[*An actor standing in the wings laughs loudly.*]

SOURWIT.

Why do you suffer that actor to stand laughing behind the scenes and interrupt your rehearsal?

MEDLEY.

Oh sir, he ought to be there. He's a-laughing in his sleeve at the Patriots. He's a very considerable character and has 200 much to do by and by.

SOURWIT.

Methinks the audience should know that, or perhaps they
may mistake him as I did and hiss him.

MEDLEY.

If they should, he's a pure impudent fellow and can stand
the hisses of them all. I chose him particularly for the part. 205
—Go on, Patriots.

FIRST PATRIOT.

Gentlemen, I think this our island of Corsica is an ill state.
I do not say we are actually in war, for that we are not, but,
however, we are threatened with it daily, and why may not
the apprehension of a war, like other evils, be worse than the 210
evil itself? For my part, this I will say, this I will venture to
say, that let what will happen, I will drink a health to peace.

MEDLEY.

This gentleman is the noisy Patriot, who drinks and roars
for his country and never does either good or harm in it.
—The next is the cautious Patriot.   215

SECOND PATRIOT.

Sir, give me your hand. There's truth in what you say, and
I will pledge you with all my soul, but remember it is all
under the rose.

THIRD PATRIOT.

Look'ee, gentlemen, my shop is my country. I always
measure the prosperity of the latter by that of the former. 220
My country is either richer or poorer, in my opinion, as my
trade rises or falls; therefore, sir, I cannot agree with you
that a war would be disserviceable. On the contrary, I think
it the only way to make my country flourish; for as I am a
sword-cutler, it would make my shop flourish, so here's to 225
war!

MEDLEY.

This is the self-interested Patriot, and now you shall hear
the fourth and last kind, which is the indolent Patriot, one
who acts as I have seen a prudent man in company fall
asleep at the beginning of a fray and never wake till the end 230
on't.

FOURTH PATRIOT (*waking*).

Here's to peace or war, I do not care which.

SOURWIT.

So this gentleman being neutral, peace has it two to one.

MEDLEY.

Perhaps neither shall have it. Perhaps I have found a way
to reconcile both parties. But go on.   235

FIRST PATRIOT.

Can anyone who is a friend to Corsica wish for war in our
present circumstances? I desire to ask you all one question:
are we not a set of miserable poor dogs?

OMNES.

Ay, ay.

THIRD PATRIOT.

That we are, sure enough. That nobody will deny.   240

Enter Quidam.

QUIDAM.

Yes, sir, I deny it. (*All start.*)   Nay, gentlemen, let me not
disturb you. I beg you will all sit down. I am come to
drink a glass with you. —Can Corsica be poor while there
is this in it? (*Lays a purse on the table.*)   Nay, be not afraid
of it, gentlemen. It is honest gold, I assure you. You are a 245
set of poor dogs, you agree. I say you are not, for this is all
yours. There! (*Pours it on the table.*)   Take it among you.

FIRST PATRIOT.

And what are we to do for it?

QUIDAM.

Only say you are rich—that's all.

OMNES.

Oh, if that be all!   *They snatch up the money.* 250

QUIDAM.

Well, sir, what is your opinion now? Tell me freely.

FIRST PATRIOT.

I will. A man may be in the wrong through ignorance, but
he's a rascal who speaks with open eyes against his conscience. I own I thought we were poor, but, sir, you have
convinced me that we are rich.   255

OMNES.

We are all convinced.

240.1. *Quidam*] Robert Walpole. See Thomas Davies, *Garrick* (London,
1780), II, 205.

QUIDAM.

> Then you are all honest fellows, and here is to your healths, and since the bottle is out, hang sorrow, cast away care, e'en take a dance, and I will play you a tune on the fiddle.

OMNES.

> Agreed.   260

FIRST PATRIOT.

> Strike up when you will, we are ready to attend your motions.

> *Dance here.* Quidam *dances out and they all dance after him.*

MEDLEY.

> Perhaps there may be something intended by this dance which you don't take.

SOURWIT.

> Ay, what prithee?   265

MEDLEY.

> Sir, everyone of these Patriots have a hole in their pockets, as Mr. Quidam the fiddler there knows, so that he intends to make them dance till all the money is fallen through, which he will pick up again and so not lose one halfpenny by his generosity; so far from it, that he will get his wine 270 for nothing, and the poor people, alas! out of their own pockets pay the whole reckoning. This, sir, I think is a very pretty pantomime trick, and an ingenious burlesque on all the *fourberies* which the great Lun has exhibited in all his entertainments. And so ends my play, my farce, or what you 275 please to call it.— [*To* Lord Dapper.] May I hope it has your lordship's approbation?

LORD DAPPER.

> Very pretty, indeed, it's very pretty.

MEDLEY.

> Then, my lord, I hope I shall have your encouragement, for

278. it's] *A–F*; 'tis *Ap.*

---

259. *take a dance*] cf. Walpole's remark on the imminent failure of the Excise Bill: "The dance it will no further go" (John Hervey, *Memoirs*, ed. J. W. Croker [London, 1884], I, 201).

274. *fourberies*] deceits.

274. *the great Lun*] John Rich.

things in this town do not always succeed according to their 280
merit. There is a vogue, my lord, which if you will bring me
into, you will lay a lasting obligation on me. And you, Mr.
Sourwit, I hope will serve me among the critics, that I may
have no elaborate treatise writ to prove that a farce of three
acts is not a regular play of five. Lastly [*addressing the audience*], 285
to you, gentlemen, whom I have not the honor to know,
who have pleased to grace my rehearsal, and you, ladies,
whether you be Shakespeare's ladies or Beaumont and
Fletcher's ladies, I hope you will make allowances for a
rehearsal: 290

> And kindly all report us to the town,
> No borrowed nor no stolen goods we've shown,
> If witty, or if dull, our play's our own.

---

288. *Shakespeare's ladies*] A blue-stocking club had been formed to pro-
mote productions of Shakespeare's plays.
288–289. *Beaumont . . . ladies*] The allusion is playful. No such organiza-
tion is known.

EURYDICE HISSED

DRAMATIS PERSONAE

SPATTER	*Mrs. Charke*
SOURWIT	*Mr. Lacy*
LORD DAPPER	*Mr. Ward*
PILLAGE	*Mr. Roberts*
HONESTUS	*Mr. Davis*
MUSE	*Mrs. Haywood*
	Mr. Blakes
	Mr. Louther
ACTORS	*Mr. Pullen*
	Mr. Topping
	Mr. Woodburn
	Mr. Machen
	Mr. Jones
GENTLEMEN	*Mr. Machen*
	Mr. Woodburn

Eurydice Hissed

or

A Word to the Wise

[*Scene: the Playhouse.*]
Enter Spatter, Sourwit, *and* Lord Dapper.

SPATTER.

My lord, I am extremely obliged to you for the honor you
show me in staying to the rehearsal of my tragedy. I hope
it will please your lordship as well as Mr. Medley's comedy
has, for I assure you 'tis ten times as ridiculous.

SOURWIT.

Is it the merit of a tragedy, Mr. Spatter, to be ridiculous?   5

SPATTER.

Yes, sir, of such tragedies as mine; and I think you, Mr.
Sourwit, will grant me this, that a tragedy had better be
ridiculous than dull, and that there is more merit in making
the audience laugh than in setting them asleep.

LORD DAPPER.

I beg, sir, you would begin, or I shan't get my hair pow-   10
dered before dinner, for I am always four hours about it.

SOURWIT.

Why, prithee, what is this tragedy of thine?

SPATTER.

Sir, it is the damnation of *Eurydice*. I fancy, Mr. Sourwit,
you will allow I have chose this subject very cunningly, for as
the town have damned my play for their own sakes, they   15
will not damn the damnation of it.

---

13. *Eurydice*] Fielding's play had failed at Drury Lane. On the evening
of its performance, February 19, 1737, a riot took place in the gallery and
the audience took exception to the character of "a ghost of a military
beau."

SOURWIT.

Faith, I must confess there is something of singular modesty in the instance.

SPATTER.

And of singular prudence too. What signifies denying the fact after sentence and dying with a lie in your mouth? No, 20
no, rather, like a good pious criminal, rejoice that in being put to shame you make some atonement for your sins. And I hope to do so in the following play, for it is, Mr. Sourwit, of a most instructive kind and conveys to us a beautiful image of the instability of human greatness and the uncer- 25
tainty of friends. You see here the author of a mighty farce at the very top and pinnacle of poetical or rather farcical greatness, followed, flattered and adored by a crowd of dependents. On a sudden, Fortune changing the scene, and his farce being damned, you see him become the scorn of his 30
admirers and deserted and abandoned by all those who courted his favor and appeared the foremost to uphold and protect him. —Draw the scene and discover Mr. Pillage.

Scene draws. [Mr. Pillage *appears on stage.*]

SOURWIT.

Who is he?

SPATTER.

The author of the farce. 35

SOURWIT.

A very odd name for an author.

SPATTER.

Perhaps you will not remain long in that opinion. But— silence!

PILLAGE.

Who'd wish to be the author of a farce,
Surrounded daily by a crowd of actors, 40
Gaping for parts and never to be satisfied;
Yet, say the wise, in loftier seats of life,
Solicitation is the chief reward,

---

33. *Pillage*] generally accepted as alluding both to Fielding and the failure of *Eurydice* and Walpole and the failure of the Excise Bill.

And Wolsey's self, that mighty minister,
In the full height and zenith of his power,   45
Amid a crowd of sycophants and slaves,
Was but perhaps the author of a farce,
Perhaps a damned one too. 'Tis all a cheat,
Some men play little farces and some great.   *Exit.*

SPATTER.
    Now for the levee.   50

SOURWIT.
    Whose levee, sir?

SPATTER.
    My poet's, sir.

SOURWIT.
    'Sdeath, sir, did ever any mortal hear of a poet's levee?

SPATTER.
    Sir, my poet is a very Great Man.

SOURWIT.
    And pray, sir, of what sort of people do you compose your   55
Great Man's levee?

SPATTER.
    Of his dependents, sir. Pray, of what sort of people are all
Great Men's levees composed? I have been forced, sir, to
do a small violence to history and make my Great Man not
only a poet but a master of a playhouse and so, sir, his levee   60
is composed of actors soliciting for parts, printers for copies,
boxkeepers, scene-men, fiddlers and candle-snuffers. And
now, Mr. Sourwit, do you think I could have composed his
levee of properer company? Come, enter, enter, gentlemen.

The levee *enters and range themselves to a ridiculous tune.*
Enter Pillage.

FIRST ACTOR.
    Sir, you have promised me a part a long time. If you had   65
not intended to employ me, it would have been kind in you
to let me know it, that I might have turned myself to some
trade or other.

    44–47. *And . . . farce*] Fielding specifically discusses these lines in *Common
Sense*, May 21, 1737.
    50. *levee*] an assembly or reception.

PILLAGE.

Sir, one farce cannot find parts for all, but you shall be pro-
vided for in time. You must have patience. I intend to ex-   70
hibit several farces. Depend on me, you shall have a part.

FIRST ACTOR.

I humbly thank you.

SECOND ACTOR.

Sir, I was to have had a principal part long ago.

PILLAGE.

Speak to me before the parts are cast and I will remember
you in my next farce. I shall exhibit several. —(*To* Third   75
Actor.) I am very glad to see you. You remember my
farce is to come on today and will lend me your hands.

THIRD ACTOR.

Depend on me.

PILLAGE [*to* Fourth Actor].

And you, sir, I hope will clap heartily.

FOURTH ACTOR.

De'el o' my sal, but I will.   80

PILLAGE.

Be sure and get into the house as soon as the doors are open.

FOURTH ACTOR.

Fear me not. I will but get a bet of denner and I will be the
first in the huse—but—

PILLAGE.

What, sir?

FOURTH ACTOR.

I want money to buy a pair of gloves.   85

PILLAGE.

I will order it you out of the office.

FOURTH ACTOR.

De'el o' my sal, but I will clap every gud thing till I bring
the huse down.

PILLAGE.

That won't do. The town of its own accord will applaud
what they like. You must stand by me when they dislike. I   90

---

80. *De'el . . . will*] perhaps an allusion to the Scottish members of Parliament who sided with Walpole.

82. *bet of denner*] bite of dinner.

don't desire any of you to clap unless when you hear a hiss. Let that be your cue for clapping.

ALL.

We'll observe.

FIFTH ACTOR.

But, sir, I have not money enough to get into the house.

PILLAGE.

I cannot disburse it. 95

FIFTH ACTOR.

But I hope you will remember your promises, sir.

PILLAGE.

Some other time. You see I am busy.— [*To* First Printer.] What are your commands, sir?

FIRST PRINTER.

I am a printer and desire to print your play.

SECOND PRINTER.

Sir, I'll give you the most money. 100

PILLAGE (*to* Second Printer, *whispering*).

You shall have it.— [*To a* Poet.] Oh! I am heartily glad to see you. (*Takes him aside.*) You know my farce comes on today and I have many enemies. I hope you will stand by me.

POET.

Depend on me, never fear your enemies. I'll warrant we 105 make more noise than they.

PILLAGE.

Thou art a very honest fellow. *Shaking him by the hand.*

POET.

I am always proud to serve you.

PILLAGE.

I wish you would let me serve you. I wish you would turn actor and accept of a part in some of my farces. 110

POET.

No, I thank you, I don't intend to come upon the stage myself, but I desire you would let me recommend this handsome, genteel young fellow [*a young man steps forward*] to act the part of a fine gentleman.

PILLAGE.

Depend on it, he shall do the very first I bring on stage. I 115 dare swear, sir, his abilities are such that the town will be obliged to us both for producing them.

POET.

> I hope so, but I must take my leave of you, for I am to meet
> a strong party that I have engaged for your service.

PILLAGE.

> Do, do. Be sure, do, clap heartily.   120

POET.

> Fear not. I warrant we bring you off triumphant.
>
> *[Members of the levee] exeunt.*

PILLAGE.

> Then I defy the town, if by my friends,
> Against their liking, I support my farce,
> And fill my loaded pockets with their pence,
> Let after-ages damn me if they please.   125

SOURWIT.

> Well, sir, and pray what do you principally intend by this
> levee scene?

SPATTER.

> Sir, I intend first to warn all future authors from depending
> solely on a party to support them against the judgment of
> the town. Secondly, showing that even the author of a farce 130
> may have his attendants and dependents, I hope greater
> persons may learn to despise them, which may be a more
> useful moral than you may apprehend; for perhaps the mean
> ambition of being worshipped, flattered, and attended by
> such fellows as these may have led men into the worst of 135
> schemes, from which they could promise themselves little
> more.

Enter Honestus.

HONESTUS.

> You sent me word that you desired to see me.

PILLAGE.

> I did, Honestus, for my farce appears
> This day upon the stage, and I entreat   140
> Your presence in the pit to help applaud it.

HONESTUS.

> Faith, sir, my voice shall never be corrupt.

141. help applaud] *A–F*; help
t'applaud *Ap.*

137.1. *Honestus*] perhaps Lord Scarborough. See John Hervey, *Memoirs,*
ed. J. W. Croker (London, 1884), I, 154.

If I approve your farce, I will applaud it:
If not, I'll hiss it, though I hiss alone.

PILLAGE.

Now, by my soul, I hope to see the time   145
When none shall dare to hiss within the house.

HONESTUS.

I rather hope to see the time when none
Shall come prepared to censure or applaud,
But merit always bear away the prize,
If you have merit, take your merit's due;   150
If not, why should a bungler in his art
Keep off some better genius from the stage?
I tell you, sir, the farce you act tonight
I don't approve, nor will the house, unless
Your friends by partiality prevail.   155
Besides, you are most impolitic to affront
The army in the beginning of your piece.
Your satire is unjust. I know no ghost
Of army beaux, unless of your own making.

SOURWIT.

What do you mean by that?   160

SPATTER.

Sir, in the farce of *Eurydice* a ghost of an army beau was
brought on the stage.

SOURWIT.

Oh, ay! I remember him.

PILLAGE.

I fear them not, I have so many friends
That the majority will sure be mine.   165

HONESTUS.

Curse on this way of carrying things by friends,
This bar to merit, by such unjust means.
A play's success or ill success is known
And fixed before it has been tried i' the house;

156–157. *Besides . . . piece*] Lord Scarborough had reported to Walpole
in 1733 that the army was disturbed by the possibility that the Excise Bill
would increase the price of tobacco.

161. *ghost . . . beau*] See note to l.13.

Yet grant it should succeed, grant that by chance   170
Or by the whim and madness of the town
A farce without contrivance, without sense,
Should run to the astonishment of mankind;
Think how you will be read in after-times,
When friends are not, and the impartial judge   175
Shall with the meanest scribbler rank your name;
Who would not rather wish a Butler's fame,
Distressed and poor in everything but merit,
Than be the blundering laureate to a court?

PILLAGE.

Not I. —On me, ye gods, bestow the pence,   180
And give your fame to any fools you please.

HONESTUS.

Your love of pence sufficiently you show
By raising still your prices on the town.

PILLAGE.

The town for their own sakes those prices pay
Which the additional expense demands.   185

HONESTUS.

Then give us a good tragedy for our money,
And let not Harlequin still pick our pockets
With his low paltry tricks and juggling cheats
Which any schoolboy, was he on the stage,
Could do as well as he. In former times,   190
When better actors acted better plays,
The town paid less.

PILLAGE.   We have more actors now.

HONESTUS.

Ay, many more, I'm certain, than you need.
Make your additional expense apparent,
Let it appear quite necessary too,   195
And then, perhaps, they'll grumble not to pay.

---

177. *Butler's fame*] Samuel Butler (1612–1680), author of *Hudibras*, died in poverty.
179. *laureate*] i.e., Colley Cibber.
183. *raising prices*] Fleetwood had recently raised the admission prices at Drury Lane.
187. *Harlequin . . . pockets*] Prices were raised for the harlequinades.

PILLAGE.

What is a manager whom the public rule?

HONESTUS.

The servant of the public and no more.
For though indeed you see the actors paid,
Yet from the people's pockets come the pence,   200
They therefore should decide what they will pay for.

PILLAGE.

If you assist me on this trial day,
You may assure yourself a dedication.

HONESTUS.

No bribe—I go impartial to your cause,   ⎫
Like a just critic to give worth applause,   ⎬   205
But damn you if you write against our laws. ⎭   *Exit.*

PILLAGE.

I wish I could have gained one honest man
Sure to my side, but since the attempt is vain,
Numbers must serve for worth; the vessel sails
With equal rapid fury and success,   210
Borne by the foulest tide as clearest stream.

Enter Valet de Chambre.

VALET.

Your honor's Muse is come to wait upon you.

PILLAGE.

Show her in.
I guess she comes to chide me for neglect,
Since twice two days have passed since I invoked her.   215

Enter Muse.

SOURWIT.

The devil there have! This is a mighty pretty way the
gentleman has found out to insinuate his acquaintance with
the muses; though, like other ladies, I believe they are often
wronged by fellows who brag of favors they never received.

PILLAGE.

Why wears my gentle Muse so stern a brow?   220

208. the attempt] *A–F*; th'attempt
Ap.

Why awful thus affects she to appear,
Where she delighted to be so serene?

MUSE.

And dost thou ask, thou traitor, dost thou ask?
Are not thou conscious of the wrongs I bear,
Neglected, slighted for a fresher Muse?   225
I, whose fond heart too easily did yield
My virgin joys and honor to thy arms
And bore thee *Pasquin*.

PILLAGE.   Where will this fury end?

MUSE.

Ask thy base heart whose is *Eurydice*?

PILLAGE.

By all that's great, begotten on no Muse,   230
The trifling offspring of an idle hour,
When you were absent, far below your care.

MUSE.

Can I believe you had her by no Muse?

PILLAGE.

Ay, by your love, and more, by mine, you shall.
My raptured fancy shall again enjoy thee,   235
Cure all thy jealousies and ease thy fears.

MUSE.

Wilt thou? Make ready then thy pen and ink.

PILLAGE.

Oh, they are ever ready; when they fail
Mayest thou forsake me, mayest thou then inspire
The blundering brain of scribblers who for hire   240
Would write away their country's liberties.

MUSE.

Oh, name not wretches so below the muse.
No, my dear Pillage, sooner will I whet
The ordinary of Newgate's leaden quill,
Sooner will I indite the annual verse   245
Which city bellmen or court laureates sing,

---

225. *Neglected ... Muse*] possibly an allusion to the fact that Walpole
neglected his wife and preferred the company of his mistress, Molly Skerett.

244. *ordinary of Newgate*] Thomas Purney, chaplain of Newgate from
1719–1727 and minor poet.

246. *city bellmen*] night watchmen and doggerel versifiers.

Sooner with thee in humble garret dwell,
And thou, or else thy muse disclaims thy pen,
Wouldst sooner starve, ay, even in prison starve,
Than vindicate oppression for thy bread,   250
Or write down liberty to gain thy own.

SOURWIT.

Heyday! Methinks this merry tragedy is growing sublime.

PATTER.

That last is, indeed, a little out of my present style. It
dropped from me before I was aware. Talking of liberty
made me serious in spite of my teeth, for between you and   255
me, Mr. Sourwit, I think that affair is past a jest. But I ask
your pardon, you shall have no more on't.

PILLAGE.

Come to my arms, inspire me with sweet thoughts,
And now thy inspiration fires my brain.
Not more I felt thy power, nor fiercer burned   260
My vigorous fancy when thy blushing charms
First yielded trembling, and inspired my pen
To write nine scenes with spirit in one day.

MUSE.

That was a day indeed!

SOURWIT.   Ay, faith! So it was!

MUSE.

And does my Pillage write with joy as then?   265
Would not a fresher subject charm his pen?

PILLAGE.

Let the dull sated appetite require
Variety to whet its blunted edge;
The subject which has once delighted me
Shall still delight, shall ever be my choice.   270
Come to my arms, thou masterpiece of nature.
The fairest rose first opening to the sun
Bears not thy beauty, nor sends forth thy sweets,
But that once gathered loses all its pride,
Fades to the sight, and sickens to the smell.   275
Thou, gathered, charmest every sense the more,
Canst flourish and be gathered o'er and o'er.

[Pillage *and the* Muse] *exeunt.*

-64-

SPATTER.

There—they are gone to write a scene, and the town may expect the fruit of it.

SOURWIT.

Yes, I think the town may expect an offspring indeed.   280

SPATTER.

But now my catastrophe is approaching. Change the scene to the outside of the playhouse and enter two gentlemen.

[*The scene draws.*] *Enter two* Gentlemen.

FIRST GENTLEMAN.

Came you from the house?

SECOND GENTLEMAN.

I did.

FIRST GENTLEMAN.

How wears the farce?   285

SECOND GENTLEMAN.

The pit is crammed, I could not get admission,
But at the door I heard a mighty noise,
It seemed of approbation and of laughter.

FIRST GENTLEMAN.

If laughter, it was surely approbation,
For I've long studied the dramatic art,   290
Read many volumes, seen a thousand plays,
Whence I've at length found out this certain truth,
That laughs applaud a farce and tears a tragedy.

SOURWIT.

A very great discovery indeed, and very pompously introduced!   295

SPATTER.

You sneer, Mr. Sourwit, but I have seen discoveries in life of the same nature introduced with much greater pomp.

SOURWIT.

But don't you intend to lay the scene in the theater and let us see the farce fairly damned before us?

---

280. *may . . . indeed*] perhaps an allusion to Walpole's natural daughter by Molly Skerett.
293. *That . . . tragedy*] cf. the Little Theatre's performance notice in *The Daily Advertiser* of March 21, 1737. See Introduction, p. xii.

SPATTER.

No, sir. It is a thing of too horrible a nature, for which 300
reason I shall follow Horace's rule and only introduce a
description of it. —Come, enter Description. I assure you I
have thrown myself out great in this next scene.

Enter Third Gentleman.

THIRD GENTLEMAN.

Oh friends, all's lost; *Eurydice* is damned.

SECOND GENTLEMAN.

Ha! Damned! A few short minutes past I came 305
From the pit-door and heard a loud applause.

THIRD GENTLEMAN.

'Tis true. At first the pit seemed greatly pleased,
And loud applauses through the benches rung,
But as the plot began to open more,
(A shallow plot) the claps less frequent grew 310
Till by degrees a gentle hiss arose;
This by a catcall from the gallery
Was quickly seconded. Then followed claps,
And long 'twixt claps and hisses did succeed
A stern contention: victory hung dubious. 315
So hangs the conscience, doubtful to determine,
When honesty pleads here and there a bribe.
At length from some ill-fated actor's mouth
Sudden there issued forth a horrid dram,
And from another rushed two gallons forth. 320
The audience, as it were contagious air,
All caught it, hallooed, catcalled, hissed and groaned.

FIRST GENTLEMAN.

I always thought, indeed, that joke would damn him,
And told him that the people would not take it.

THIRD GENTLEMAN.

But it was mighty pleasant to behold, 325
When the damnation of the farce was sure,
How all those friends who had begun the claps

---

301. *Horace's rule*] *Ars Poetica*, ll. 179–188.
307–329. *At first . . . disapprobation*] a description both of the failure of
Eurydice and the failure of the Excise Bill on its second reading.

With greatest vigor strove who first should hiss
And show disapprobation. And John Watts
Who was this morning eager for the copy,   330
Slunk hasty from the pit and shook his head.

SECOND GENTLEMAN.
And so 'tis certain that his farce is gone?

THIRD GENTLEMAN.
Most certain.

SECOND GENTLEMAN. Let us then retire with speed,
For see he comes this way.

THIRD GENTLEMAN.   By all means
Let us avoid him with what haste we can.   335

[*The* Three Gentlemen] *exeunt.*

Enter Pillage.

PILLAGE.
Then I am damned. Cursed henceforth be the bard
Whoe'er depends on fortune or on friends.

SOURWIT.
So, the play is over, for I reckon you will not find it possible
to get anyone to come near this honest gentleman.

SPATTER.
Yes, sir, there is one, and you may easily guess who it is. 340
The man who will not flatter his friend in prosperity will
hardly leave him in adversity. —Come, enter Honestus.

[*Enter* Honestus.]

PILLAGE.
Honestus here! Will he not shun me too?

HONESTUS.
When *Pasquin* run and the town liked you most,
And every scribbler loaded you with praise,   345
I did not court you, nor will shun you now.

PILLAGE.
Oh, had I taken your advice, my friend,
I had not now been damned! Then had I trusted
To the impartial judgment of the town,
And by the goodness of my piece had tried   350

---

329. *John Watts*] publisher of many of Fielding's plays. *Eurydice* was published for the first time in Fielding's *Miscellanies* (1743).

To merit favor, nor with vain reliance
On the frail promise of uncertain friends
Produced a farce like this—friends who forsook me,
And left me nought to comfort me but this.   *Drinks.*

HONESTUS.

Forbear to drink.

PILLAGE.   Oh, it is now too late!   355
Already I have drank two bottles off
Of this fell potion and it now begins
To work its deadly purpose on my brain.
I'm giddy. Ha! My head begins to swim,
And see Eurydice all pale before me.   360
Why dost thou haunt me thus? I did not damn thee.
By Jove, there never was a better farce.
She beckons me—say—whether—blame the town
And not thy Pillage. —Now my brain's on fire!
My staggering senses dance and I am—

HONESTUS.   Drunk.   365
That word he should have said that ends the verse.
Farewell, a twelve hours nap compose thy senses.
May mankind profit by thy sad example.
May men grow wiser, writers grow more scarce,
And no man dare to make a simple farce.   370

FINIS

---

356. *drank . . . off*] perhaps an ironical allusion to Walpole's drinking and the unpopular Gin Act of 1736.

359–364. *I'm giddy . . . fire*] These lines recall Belvidera's mad scene in Act V of Otway's *Venice Preserved.*

Appendix

Chronology

Approximate years are indicated by *. Dates for plays are those on which they were first made public, either on stage or in print.

Political and Literary Events	Life and Major Works of Fielding
1631 Death of Donne. John Dryden born.	
1633 Samuel Pepys born.	
1635 Sir George Etherege born.*	
1640 Aphra Behn born.*	
1641 William Wycherley born.*	
1642 First Civil War began (ended 1646). Theaters closed by Parliament. Thomas Shadwell born.*	
1648 Second Civil War.	
1649 Execution of Charles I.	
1650 Jeremy Collier born.	
1651 Hobbes' *Leviathan* published.	
1652 First Dutch War began (ended 1654). Thomas Otway born.	

1653
Nathaniel Lee born.*

1656
D'Avenant's *THE SIEGE OF RHODES* performed at Rutland House.

1657
John Dennis born.

1658
Death of Oliver Cromwell.
D'Avenant's *THE CRUELTY OF THE SPANIARDS IN PERU* performed at the Cockpit.

1660
Restoration of Charles II.
Theatrical patents granted to Thomas Killigrew and Sir William D'Avenant, authorizing them to form, respectively, the King's and the Duke of York's Companies.
Pepys began his diary.

1661
Cowley's *THE CUTTER OF COLEMAN STREET*.
D'Avenant's *THE SIEGE OF RHODES* (expanded to two parts).

1662
Charter granted to the Royal Society.

1663
Dryden's *THE WILD GALLANT*.
Tuke's *THE ADVENTURES OF FIVE HOURS*.

1664
Sir John Vanbrugh born.
Dryden's *THE RIVAL LADIES*.
Dryden and Howard's *THE INDIAN QUEEN*.
Etherege's *THE COMICAL REVENGE*.

1665
Second Dutch War began (ended 1667).

Great Plague.
Dryden's *THE INDIAN EM-
PEROR*
Orrery's *MUSTAPHA.*

1666
Fire of London.
Death of James Shirley.

1667
Jonathan Swift born.
Milton's *Paradise Lost* published.
Sprat's *The History of the Royal
Society* published.
Dryden's *SECRET LOVE.*

1668
Death of D'Avenant.
Dryden made Poet Laureate.
Dryden's *An Essay of Dramatic
Poesy* published.
Shadwell's *THE SULLEN
LOVERS.*

1669
Pepys terminated his diary.
Susannah Centlivre born.

1670
William Congreve born.
Dryden's *THE CONQUEST OF
GRANADA*, Part I.

1671
Dorset Garden Theatre (Duke's
Company) opened.
Colley Cibber born.
Milton's *Paradise Regained* and *Sam-
son Agonistes* published.
Dryden's *THE CONQUEST OF
GRANADA*, Part II.
THE REHEARSAL, by the Duke
of Buckingham and others.
Wycherley's *LOVE IN A WOOD.*

1672
Third Dutch War began (ended
1674).

7

Joseph Addison born.
Richard Steele born.
Dryden's *MARRIAGE À LA MODE.*

1674
New Drury Lane Theatre (King's Company) opened.
Death of Milton.
Nicholas Rowe born.
Thomas Rymer's *Reflections on Aristotle's Treatise of Poesy* (translation of Rapin) published.

1675
Dryden's *AURENG-ZEBE.*
Wycherley's *THE COUNTRY WIFE.*

1676
Etherege's *THE MAN OF MODE.*
Otway's *DON CARLOS.*
Shadwell's *THE VIRTUOSO.*
Wycherley's *THE PLAIN DEALER.*

1677
Rymer's *Tragedies of the Last Age Considered* published.
Aphra Behn's *THE ROVER.*
Dryden's *ALL FOR LOVE.*
Lee's *THE RIVAL QUEENS.*

1678
Popish Plot.
George Farquhar born.
Bunyan's *Pilgrim's Progress* (Part I) published.

1679
Exclusion Bill introduced.
Death of Thomas Hobbes.
Death of Roger Boyle, Earl of Orrery.
Charles Johnson born.

1680
Death of Samuel Butler.
Death of John Wilmot, Earl of Rochester.

Dryden's *THE SPANISH FRIAR.*
Lee's *LUCIUS JUNIUS BRUTUS.*
Otway's *THE ORPHAN.*

1681
Charles II dissolved Parliament at
Oxford.
Dryden's *Absalom and Achitophel* published.
Tate's adaptation of *KING LEAR.*

1682
The King's and Duke of York's
Companies merged into the United
Company.
Dryden's *The Medal, MacFlecknoe,*
and *Religio Laici* published.
Otway's *VENICE PRESERVED.*

1683
Rye House Plot.
Death of Thomas Killigrew.
Crowne's *CITY POLITIQUES.*

1685
Death of Charles II; accession of
James II.
Revocation of the Edict of Nantes.
The Duke of Monmouth's Rebellion.
Death of Otway.
John Gay born.
Crowne's *SIR COURTLY NICE.*
Dryden's *ALBION AND ALBANIUS.*

1687
Death of the Duke of Buckingham.
Dryden's *The Hind and the Panther*
published.
Newton's *Principia* published.

1688
The Revolution.
Alexander Pope born.
Shadwell's *THE SQUIRE OF
ALSATIA.*

1689

The War of the League of Augsburg
began (ended 1697).

Toleration Act.

Death of Aphra Behn.

Shadwell made Poet Laureate.

Dryden's *DON SEBASTIAN*.

Shadwell's *BURY FAIR*.

1690

Battle of the Boyne.

Locke's *Two Treatises of Government*
and *An Essay Concerning Human
Understanding* published.

1691

Death of Etherege.*

Langbaine's *An Account of the English
Dramatic Poets* published.

1692

Death of Lee.

Death of Shadwell.

Tate made Poet Laureate.

1693

George Lillo born.*

Rymer's *A Short View of Tragedy*
published.

Congreve's *THE OLD BACHELOR*.

1694

Death of Queen Mary.

Southerne's *THE FATAL MAR-
RIAGE*.

1695

Group of actors led by Thomas
Betterton left Drury Lane and
established a new company at
Lincoln's Inn Fields.

Congreve's *LOVE FOR LOVE*.

Southerne's *OROONOKO*.

1696

Cibber's *LOVE'S LAST SHIFT*.

Vanbrugh's *THE RELAPSE*.

1697

Treaty of Ryswick ended the War
of the League of Augsburg.

Charles Macklin born.

Congreve's *THE MOURNING BRIDE*.

Vanbrugh's *THE PROVOKED WIFE*.

1698

Collier controversy started with the publication of *A Short View of the Immorality and Profaneness of the English Stage*.

1699

Farquhar's *THE CONSTANT COUPLE*.

1700

Death of Dryden.

Blackmore's *Satire against Wit* published.

Congreve's *THE WAY OF THE WORLD*.

1701

Act of Settlement.

War of the Spanish Succession began (ended 1713).

Death of James II.

Rowe's *TAMERLANE*.

Steele's *THE FUNERAL*.

1702

Death of William III; accession of Anne.

The Daily Courant began publication.

Cibber's *SHE WOULD AND SHE WOULD NOT*.

1703

Death of Samuel Pepys.

Rowe's *THE FAIR PENITENT*.

1704

Capture of Gibraltar; Battle of Blenheim.

Defoe's *The Review* began publication (1704–1713).

Swift's *A Tale of a Tub* and *The Battle of the Books* published.

Cibber's *THE CARELESS HUS-BAND.*

1705

Haymarket Theatre opened.

Steele's *THE TENDER HUS-BAND.*

1706

Battle of Ramillies.

Farquhar's *THE RECRUITING OFFICER.*

1707

Union of Scotland and England.   Born April 22.

Death of Farquhar.

Farquhar's *THE BEAUX' STRATAGEM.*

1708

Downes' *Roscius Anglicanus* published.

1709

Samuel Johnson born.

Rowe's edition of Shakespeare published.

The Tatler began publication (1709–1711).

Centlivre's *THE BUSY BODY.*

1711

Shaftesbury's *Characteristics* published.

The Spectator began publication (1711–1712).

Pope's *An Essay on Criticism* published.

1713

Treaty of Utrecht ended the War of the Spanish Succession.

Addison's *CATO.*

1714

Death of Anne; accession of George I.

Steele became Governor of Drury Lane.

John Rich assumed management of Lincoln's Inn Fields.

Centlivre's *THE WONDER: A WOMAN KEEPS A SECRET.*
Rowe's *JANE SHORE.*

1715
Jacobite Rebellion.
Death of Tate.
Rowe made Poet Laureate.
Death of Wycherley.

1716
Addison's *THE DRUMMER.*

1717
David Garrick born.
Cibber's *THE NON-JUROR.*
Gay, Pope, and Arbuthnot's *THREE HOURS AFTER MARRIAGE.*

1718
Death of Rowe.
Centlivre's *A BOLD STROKE FOR A WIFE.*

1719
Death of Addison.
Defoe's *Robinson Crusoe* published.
Young's *BUSIRIS, KING OF EGYPT.*

Entered Eton; remained there until 1725.*

1720
South Sea Bubble.
Samuel Foote born.
Little Theatre in the Haymarket opened. Steele suspended from the Governorship of Drury Lane (restored 1721).
Steele's *The Theatre* published.
Hughes' *THE SIEGE OF DAMASCUS.*

1721
Walpole became first Minister.

1722
Steele's *THE CONSCIOUS LOVERS.*

1723
Death of Susannah Centlivre.

Death of D'Urfey.

1725

Pope's edition of Shakespeare published.

1726

Death of Jeremy Collier.

Death of Vanbrugh.

Law's *Unlawfulness of Stage Entertainments* published.

Swift's *Gulliver's Travels* published.

1727

Death of George I; accession of George II.

Death of Sir Isaac Newton.

Arthur Murphy born.

1728

Pope's *The Dunciad* (first version) published.

Cibber's *THE PROVOKED HUSBAND* (expansion of Vanbrugh's fragment *A JOURNEY TO LONDON*).

Gay's *THE BEGGAR'S OPERA*.

The Masquerade published.
LOVE IN SEVERAL MASQUES (Drury Lane, February 16).
Enrolled at the University of Leyden.

1729

Goodman's Fields Theatre opened.

Death of Congreve.

Death of Steele.

Edmund Burke born.

Returned from Leyden.

1730

Cibber made Poet Laureate.

Oliver Goldsmith born.

Thomson's *The Seasons* published.

THE TEMPLE BEAU (Goodman's Fields, January 26).
THE AUTHOR'S FARCE (Haymarket, March 30).
TOM THUMB (Haymarket, April 24).
RAPE UPON RAPE (Haymarket, June 23).

1731

Death of Defoe.

Lillo's *THE LONDON MERCHANT*.

THE LETTER WRITERS (Haymarket, March 24).
THE TRAGEDY OF TRAGEDIES [revision of *TOM THUMB*] (Haymarket, March 24).

THE WELSH OPERA (Haymarket, April 22), revised as THE GRUB-STREET OPERA (suppressed).

1732

Covent Garden Theatre opened.
Death of Gay.
George Colman the elder born.
Charles Johnson's CAELIA.

THE LOTTERY (Drury Lane, January 1).
THE MODERN HUSBAND (Drury Lane, February 14).
THE OLD DEBAUCHEES (Drury Lane, June 1).
THE COVENT GARDEN TRAGEDY (Drury Lane, June 1).
THE MOCK DOCTOR (Drury Lane, June 23).

1733

Pope's An Essay on Man (Epistles I–III) published (Epistle IV, 1734).

THE MISER (Drury Lane, February 17).

1734

Death of Dennis.
The Prompter began publication (1734–1736).
Theobald's edition of Shakespeare published.

THE AUTHOR'S FARCE, revised (Drury Lane, January 15).
THE INTRIGUING CHAMBER-MAID (Drury Lane, January 15).
DON QUIXOTE IN ENGLAND (Haymarket, April 5).
Married Charlotte Cradock, November 28.

1735

Pope's Epistle to Dr. Arbuthnot published.

AN OLD MAN TAUGHT WISDOM (Drury Lane, January 6).
THE UNIVERSAL GALLANT (Drury Lane, February 10).

1736

Lillo's FATAL CURIOSITY.

Organized "Great Mogul's Company of Comedians" at the Haymarket.
PASQUIN (Haymarket, March 5).
TUMBLE-DOWN DICK (Haymarket, April 29).

1737

The Stage Licensing Act.
Dodsley's THE KING AND THE MILLER OF MANSFIELD.

EURYDICE (Drury Lane, February 19).
THE HISTORICAL REGISTER FOR 1736 (Haymarket, March 21).

EURYDICE HISSED (Haymarket, April 13).
Entered the Middle Temple, November 1.

1738
Johnson's *London* published.
Pope's *One Thousand Seven Hundred and Thirty-Eight* published.
Thomson's *AGAMEMNON.*

1739
War with Spain began.
Death of Lillo.
Hugh Kelly born.
Johnson's *Complete Vindication of Licensers of the Stage*, an ironical criticism of the Licensing Act, published after Brooke's *GUSTAVUS VASA* was denied a license.

The Champion began publication (1739–1741).

1740
War of the Austrian Succession began (ended 1748).
James Boswell born.
Cibber's *Apology for His Life* published.
Richardson's *Pamela* published.
Garrick's *LETHE.*
Thomson and Mallet's *ALFRED.*

Called to the bar, June 20.

1741
Edmund Malone born.
Garrick began acting.
Garrick's *THE LYING VALET.*

Shamela published.

1742
Walpole resigned his offices.
Cibber's *Letters to Mr. Pope* published.
Pope's *New Dunciad* (Book IV of *The Dunciad*) published.
Young's *The Complaint, or Night Thoughts* published (additional parts published each year until 1745).

Joseph Andrews published.
MISS LUCY IN TOWN (Drury Lane, May 6).

1743
Death of Henry Carey.

Miscellanies published.

Pope's *The Dunciad* (final version) published.

1744
Death of Pope.
Death of Theobald.
Dodsley's *A Select Collection of Old Plays* published.
Johnson's *Life of Mr. Richard Savage* published.

1745
Jacobite Rebellion.
Death of Swift.
Thomas Holcroft born.
Johnson's *Observations on Macbeth* published.
Thomson's *TANCRED AND SIGISMUNDA*.

1746
Death of Southerne.
Collins's *Odes* published.

1747
Garrick entered the management of Drury Lane Theatre.
Johnson's *Prologue Spoken by Mr. Garrick at the Opening of the Theatre in Drury Lane, 1747*.
Warburton's edition of Shakespeare published.
Garrick's *MISS IN HER TEENS*.
Hoadly's *THE SUSPICIOUS HUS-BAND*.

1748
Treaty of Aix-la-Chapelle ended the War of the Austrian Succession.
Death of Thomson.
Hume's *Philosophical Essays Concerning Human Understanding* published.
Richardson's *Clarissa* published.
Smollett's *Roderick Random* published.

1749
Death of Ambrose Philips.

THE WEDDING DAY (Drury Lane, February 17).
Death of his wife.*

Married Mary Daniel, November 27.

Appointed Justice of Peace for Westminster.

Tom Jones published.

Bolingbroke's *Idea of a Patriot King*
published.
Chetwood's *A General History of the
Stage* published.
Johnson's *The Vanity of Human
Wishes* published.
Hill's *MEROPE* (adaptation of
Voltaire).
Johnson's *IRENE*.

1750
Death of Aaron Hill.
Johnson's *The Rambler* began publi-
cation (1750–1752).

1751
Death of Bolingbroke.
Richard Brinsley Sheridan born.
Gray's *An Elegy Wrote in a Country
Churchyard* published.
Smollett's *Peregrine Pickle* published.

1752
Mason's *ELFRIDA* published.

Amelia published.
The Covent Garden Journal published.

1753
Death of Bishop Berkeley.
Elizabeth Inchbald born.
Foote's *THE ENGLISHMAN IN
PARIS*.
Glover's *BOADICEA*.
Moore's *THE GAMESTER*.
Young's *THE BROTHERS*.

1754
Richardson's *Sir Charles Grandison*
published.
Whitehead's *CREUSA, QUEEN OF
ATHENS*.

Died in Lisbon, October 8.

1755
Johnson's *A Dictionary of the English
Language* published.
John Brown's *BARBAROSSA*.

Journal of a Voyage to Lisbon published.

1756
Seven Years War began.
William Godwin born.

Burke's *A Philosophical Enquiry into
... the Sublime and Beautiful* published.

First part of Joseph Warton's *Essay
on ... Pope* published (second part, 1782).

Murphy's *THE APPRENTICE.*

1757

Battle of Plassey (India).
Death of Cibber.
Death of Moore.
William Blake born.
Gray's *Odes* published.
Home's *DOUGLAS* (performed the
year before in Edinburgh).